THE
PRIVILEGE
RACE

THE
PRIVILEGE
RACE

*A Guide to Overcoming
Negative Voices and Influences*

BRIAN THOMAS

Forefront
BOOKS

Published by Forefront Books.
Distributed by Simon & Schuster.

Library of Congress Control Number: 2023918131

Print ISBN: 978-1-63763-203-1
E-book ISBN: 978-1-63763-204-8

Cover Design by Bruce Gore, Gore Studio, Inc.
Interior Design by Mary Susan Oleson, BLU Design Concepts

For my parents... for making decisions and working hard for more opportunity and a better life for their children. I would not have this awesome life without the decisions they made over forty years ago.

Contents

Foreword

I'm inspired to write this foreword for Brian, not simply because he asked (which was an honor and privilege), but because I deeply believe in the core message of the book: your life today is a product of your decisions, not your circumstances, and you alone have the power to overcome your limitations and create the life of your dreams.

I first met Brian in 2020 when he emailed me out of the blue one Friday evening. I host a personal development podcast and coach people on "having it all," and as a long-time listener Brian wanted to share his gratitude for the show and the breakthroughs he'd recently experienced. His email was vulnerable, self-reflective and sincere, and he ended it with a simple request: for guidance and accountability.

Over the following years I honored Brian's request, guiding him on how to live his life in harmony with his principles and values, and holding him accountable to facing his deepest fears and most limiting beliefs.

I remember one coaching conversation where Brian shared that he was interested in doing a 24-hour fitness challenge but was hesitant to commit because of the physical toll the challenge would take on his body. Brian's beliefs around his physical capacity were creating fear and doubt that I could clearly see were feeding a very limiting story he held about himself. What's revealing about this conversation is that it highlights Brian's deep commitment to self-improvement. He knew that if he brought the idea of the physical challenge to me, that I would absolutely hold him accountable for picking a date and getting it done.

It can be incredibly difficult and confronting to face yourself, because to do that means you must grapple with your deepest beliefs about who you are and how the world works. Brian has been willing to step into that arena again and again, and that's why, like his hero Rocky Balboa, he is able to rise up after life punches him in the mouth.

And that's what I find most inspiring about Brian.

The Privilege Race is ultimately the story of Brian's journey of facing himself: the stories of his past, the realities of his present, and the possibilities of his future.

I invite you to read the following pages with an open heart and with the belief that we are all connected, no matter our backgrounds. Whether you share obvious commonalities with Brian or not, you are connected by the simple fact that you are a human being doing the best you can to navigate life's ups and downs.

This book will help you—another intrepid soul on a journey of self-discovery and mastery—to face your dragons with courage, confidence and humility. In each of its stories is a relatable lesson to draw wisdom from. In each of its chapters are concrete takeaways that can be applied in practical and simple ways.

Let this book guide you out of the judgment, anger and victimhood that might be coloring your current life's experience, and bring you to a state of love, courage and intentionality that can propel you to incredible heights.

Brian's life story has inspired me to look at my journey in new ways, and I pray that it does the same for you.

Much Love,

Matthew Bivens
HOST OF THE HAVING IT A.L.L. PODCAST

CHAPTER ONE

The Introduction to Your New Future

It was a beautiful June day—80 degrees and sunny, with a few wisps of clouds. I was out for an 8:00 a.m. walk. Kids were still sleeping as summer vacation had begun earlier in the week. The sidewalk was damp from neighbors watering their lawns, and people were not yet clogging the roads and sidewalks. Birds were singing, squirrels were playing, bunnies were eating flowers. It was a perfect summer morning.

Though I was walking in that perfection, had you looked at me, you would have seen me crying. It was one of those cries when you're in public and you're trying to hold it together. The cry that you get at a movie and you don't want anyone to know you're crying and then the lights come on and you're like, "I'm good; I'm good!"

The cry was because I had freed something that had been within me for decades. And with that release, an emotional wave overwhelmed my body. I started to soar as I walked the damp concrete. It felt as if I were being carried into the palm of a big hand that guided me along on my walk. Perhaps the hand was there all the time, but for those moments that morning, I got to feel it.

For decades I told myself I was defective. I told myself I could not do physical things because of my limitations. I could not play baseball, football, run, golf, skate, swim, rollerblade, work out my legs. My mother had told me these things as a child—for good reason. Because of my kidney disease, I was treated as flawed and fragile. And the mindset that followed me around daily for decades—and still does—was saturated in fragility. *Be careful! Don't do that! Protect yourself! Watch out!* I grew up on constant patrol, as though I were my own lifeguard endlessly watching over me. Not only was it exhausting, but by saying no to myself for decades, I grew to believe I couldn't do things.

All of those things I could not physically do bled into my psyche, bled into *me*. That constant questioning impacted things outside of my physical limitations: I wondered if I would finish law school, date a particular girl, get married and have a family, buy the home I wanted, buy the car I wanted, practice law, run a business, own a business, write a book … that list was infinite. I constantly reminded myself that I was defective. When a friend didn't return a phone call, it was because I was defective. If a friend didn't initiate a phone call, it was because I was defective.

I have had two kidney transplants—one when I was thirteen years old and the second nineteen years later when I was thirty-two. Both kidney transplants led to pretty significant hip issues that required three surgeries in my teens. I need two hip replacements. The last time I saw an orthopedic surgeon, the doctor looked at X-rays in front of me, gawked, and summoned what felt like forty-two medical students into my little exam room to show them an example of messed-up hips. Great! My hips made me a circus freak.

I have limited range of motion in my hips and I lack strength in my hips and pelvis. Walking has been painful. I do not run because of the pain and impact it has on my hips. In the past, I have forced myself to coach my daughter's softball teams, but the day before games and practices I did little physically so I would be able to move around with them. The day after practices and games I was inactive in order to recover. My brain naturally put this switch on me because of my hips, and I unhappily acquiesced to those limitations. "Defective" and "limited" was how I viewed myself.

In the months before this particular June day, my life coach, Matthew Bivens, suggested that I work on ways to give myself more mobility around my hip function. He asked me to think of some things I could do to help my hips. At that time, walking a mile was tough because of pain. So he asked a very simple question: rather than sitting in pain all the time, what are some options you have to alleviate it?

"I could stretch—but even when I do, it doesn't help," I said.

"Are you stretching the right things? Could you enlist some professional help to get that question answered?" he asked.

That led to the one-week goal of contacting a physical therapist and scheduling an appointment. I contacted Amy Goldstein and explained how my hips were bone on bone and that I was a hip replacement candidate but did not want to have those surgeries. She did an assessment by making me move—or try to move—in certain ways. She came to some conclusions and started a treatment plan. That treatment changed my life. She encouraged me to perform little stretches that took ten to fifteen minutes to complete, and my pain level went down dramatically. I was able to walk in much less pain, and when I did have pain, I had strategies to alleviate it. I could go to softball with my daughter and stretch afterward and find myself functional the next day.

Amy also referred me to a trainer, Michael Hanover. His job has been to strengthen my legs so that I'll be able to easily slam-dunk over my twelve-year-old son on an eight-foot rim (okay, that's *my* goal, but better stated, he strengthens my very weak lower body muscles that have not fired in over a decade). My ego hates these workouts because I'm doing less than what my nine-year-old daughter can do. My legs feel like jelly afterward. But I continue going because I know that doing this work will get me to the goal of slam-dunking on a twelve-year-old, which functionally means being able to move with strength and without pain.

When I found myself walking down my block bawling, it was because I had started to release that definition of myself being fragile and a victim of my hips. That belief had impacted me for the last eighteen years. That belief—that truth I held about myself—lifted. I let go of the weight I carried consciously and subconsciously. It was a powerful moment.

Putting in the Work

David Goggins is a retired Navy SEAL and current ultra-marathoner. He may best be described as America's most fit person. Goggins has done many incredible, almost unhuman, physical feats, starting with the San Diego One Day where he ran/walked one hundred miles in twenty-four hours. He's done the Badwater Ultra Marathon several times and the McNaughton 150 Miler (which he won), and he holds the record for the number of pulls-ups done in twenty-four hours (4,030 in seventeen hours). In short, he's badass.[1]

David Goggins "invented" the Goggins 4 x 4 x 48 Challenge.[2] I first learned about it when my friend Mark Livingston did it. His wife left town to visit her sister and he decided—on a whim—to run four miles every four hours for forty-eight hours. His "screw it, I'm going to do the Goggins" mentality stuck with me for months. My brain kept telling me I could never do such a thing—hell, I could barely walk a mile! Maybe Mark's casual decision to give it a shot affected me precisely because I knew it would be damn near impossible for me to do.

Then again, maybe it *wasn't* impossible, and I was guilty of underindexing my life. I continued not to do things I wanted to do because I believed I was not capable of it. I had become a prisoner of my own beliefs. I fell asleep each night tolerating the life I had rather than reaching for the life I *wanted*. I stayed in my comfort zone rather than challenging myself. Yet not only was there a quiet desperation for *more*, there was this feeling, this knowledge somewhere deep within, that I could have it.

And so, with the notion of having underindexed my life echoing in my mind, I decided to challenge myself. I knew that my hips would not allow me to do the 4 x 4 x 48—but could I modify it into something still challenging but doable? I could, and I did, turning this challenge into a 2 + 200 x 4 x 24: two miles plus 200 push-ups every four hours for twenty-four hours. By the end of the day, my goal was to have walked twelve miles and done 1,200 push-ups.

Thanks to Amy Goldstein, I was able to go on two-mile walks with much less pain. But would I be able to manage twelve miles? The thought of it scared me. Even if I did it, how functional would I be the next day? Would I be in bed for days recovering? Would I be popping Advil or go straight to scotch? Was it really necessary to put myself through this?

My life coach, Matthew Bivens, told me to schedule it, and when the appointed time came, I did circuits at 8:00 p.m., 12:00 a.m., 4:00 a.m., and 8:00 a.m., by which point my body was pretty sore and stiff. On that 8:00 a.m. walk, it wasn't difficult for my brain to find pain, stiffness, and inflammation in my broken-down hips. *But what's one step and then another one and another one?* I thought. *Let's just get out there and do one step at a time.*

As I started walking that fourth circuit, I was overwhelmed with stiffness in my hips and pelvis; I was coming up against a wall. I needed something to distract me, so I hit Shuffle on iTunes, and out of thousands of songs, the trumpets from "Gonna Fly Now" (the theme from *Rocky*) started blaring.

Rocky Balboa is my hero. He was barely making ends meet as a boxer when an opportunity arose for him to fight the champ, Apollo Creed. His goal in that fight wasn't to win;

it was to still be on his feet at the end of the fight. Rocky expected to get knocked down, but he vowed to keep getting up. That resonates with me.

Almost everyone knows the scene in *Rocky* where he climbs the steps of the Philadelphia Museum of Art and jumps for joy. But that's at the end of his training. The first time he climbs the stairs to that famous spot, he limps, staggers, huffs, and puffs to reach the top. Once he reaches the top, he turns around and we get a glimpse of his face, and he seems to be thinking, *What did I get myself into?* as he lets out a slight whimper, groans, holds his side, and starts to slowly and painfully make it down the steps.

YOUR FUTURE WILL CHANGE BASED ON HOW YOU VIEW YOUR PRESENT.

Juxtapose that moment of doubt and pain with the triumphant one where he bounds up the steps, raises his hands in victory, and dances. In that moment, Rocky's fight with Apollo Creed almost doesn't even matter anymore. In that moment, Rocky has won by defeating his self-doubt.

On the sidewalk that morning, I was *swimming* in self-doubt. My hips and pelvis were inflamed and the thought of walking a mere two-mile loop seemed overwhelming.

But I put one foot in front of the other. And as the *Rocky* theme played, a feeling of calm washed over me, a sense that everything was going to be all right. The wind hit my back and a voice within me said, *You. Will. Not. Fail.*

And I started bawling. I suddenly felt a burden lifted off my back. I felt light, like I was walking on air. I had just been wondering if I was going to be able to walk, and now I felt like I could go on for a hundred miles.

I. Would. Not. Fail.

In that moment, I stopped viewing myself as limited. I stopped seeing myself as fragile. In that moment, "I can't" didn't exist.

Of course, I still see myself as limited. Of course, I still sometimes say to myself, "I can't do that." My goal isn't necessarily to stop saying to myself what I've said for forty years, but rather to recognize when I do that and shift my thinking. It is putting me back on that sidewalk and remembering, *I will not fail.*

Change Your Future by Redefining Your Present

My future was impacted by that walk and the work I did to prepare for it. I made different decisions so I would be less affected by my hips. In making those decisions, I related differently to my hips. I stopped limiting myself with "I can't" and started doing things I wanted to do.

I am not special. We can all do this work. We all carry burdens with us, and we all limit ourselves by those burdens. The first step is to acknowledge the burdens we place on ourselves. Throughout this book, my goal is to throw cold water on you and wake you up. To give you the keys to find and unlock the limitations you have unintentionally shackled yourself with. You. Will. Not. Fail.

When you wake up to how you view yourself and, more importantly, why you view yourself that way, you empower yourself to change the way you view yourself, make different decisions, and gain different outcomes. And although these concepts apply to every person, let's apply it to the Black experience in America as we examine how our particular conditioning can affect us differently.

Let me begin by asking, How do you view yourself?

Do you define yourself as a mother? A social worker? A daughter? A son? A brother or sister?

Do you view yourself as a Black man? As someone who's always struggling? As unintelligent? As unhealthy? As over-weight? As a victim of racism? As a victim of circumstance?

Do you view yourself as a millionaire? As an athlete? As a landlord? As an investor? As a small business owner? As a businesswoman?

Take a moment to think about how you view yourself today and then who you see yourself as in five years. Who do you want to be in five years? Then, using a simple "I am" statement, start calling yourself that—"I am an athlete"; "I am healthy"; "I am confident"; "I am wealthy."

WHATEVER YOU BELIEVE TO BE TRUE WILL COME TRUE—SO TO BECOME MORE POWERFUL, *BELIEVE* SOMETHING THAT MAKES YOU MORE POWERFUL.

Whatever you believe to be true will come true—so to become more powerful, *believe* something that makes you more powerful. If your present mindset tells you that race has always been a prominent part of your life and you just can't escape racism in the United States, then your circumstances will flow from that present. You will find examples of being limited by the white supremacist country in which you live. Those examples are easy enough to find in the media, in our neighborhoods, and in our daily lives. By contrast, if your present perception is that you live in a time and place of educational and economic opportunity and empowerment, then you will find educational and economic opportunity and empowerment.

Whatever you believe to be true will come true—so to become more powerful, *believe* something that makes you more powerful. Racism takes our power away. Racism tells us that we can't, we're less than, that we don't deserve certain things. We subconsciously believe what we've been told for centuries. Because of those beliefs, we limit our lives and the lives of our loved ones. Decide that you, not racism, will define who you are. Visualize your positive future and you will breathe life into the person you want to become.

What you think you deserve today will dictate who you become in the future. If you subconsciously think you are not intelligent, you will subconsciously make decisions that don't use your intelligence. If you think you deserve to go to college, you'll make choices that will put you in a position to do that. Shift your self-perception and see how life changes.

After all, what do you have to lose?

CHAPTER TWO

Being Conscious of the Decisions We Make

If you don't know where you're going,
you can end up anywhere.
—George Mumford

I AM NAKED *on a cold, hard table. I shiver in the frigid air, with only a threadbare sheet over me. The smell of hospital bleach envelops me. A bunch of masked adults encircle me and shine a light on my face. My right arm grows cold; they're pumping some solution into me and telling me to count down from ten.*

Ten. Will these be my last thoughts? Am I going to die here? The table is cold and hard. My arm is cold. I'm going to stay awake and prove they can't put me to sleep. I love the summer. I can't wait to run in the summer. I love running in the sprinkler.

Nine. I'll have my body back! I'll be a kid again!

I'll be able to run and jump and play with my friends again, to feel the grass between my toes! I look forward to not being exhausted after walking a few blocks. I look forward to not being afraid.

Eight. I love my mom. I love my dad. I love my sister. I love my friends. I love my room. I feel safe in my room. I hope to get to see my room again. These guys aren't going to mess up—are they? I should get back home, right? I am concerned. But I am not afraid. I'm hopeful. This room is cold. I'm getting sleepy. But I'll stay awake! But it really is hard to keep my eyes open. Maybe I'll just close them. NO! I WILL PROVE THESE SUCKERS WRONG!

Seven. I am running, smiling, jumping. I get another chance at life. I am smiling . . . I am laughing . . . I am tired, but not the way I . . .

have been tired . . . I am sleepy . . .

I am happy . . . I get . . .

another . . .

chance . . .

It was November 5, 1986. I was a thirteen-year-old boy on an operating table at the University of Chicago. Doctors in another room had a man's kidney ready to put into my tiny body. Just six days earlier, I had gone trick-or-treating with my friends, but I couldn't keep up. I was so tired that I went home early, dragging my body through throngs of screaming kids. My mom asked why I was home so soon, but she already knew the answer: I just couldn't do it. I felt like an eighty-year-old man.

That night I cried myself to sleep in my mother's arms. It was tough to realize my body was failing me at only thirteen years old. I thought of all the things I physically could not do. The overwhelming fatigue in doing routine activities. I did not have the energy to be a boy—creating a chasm not only with my friends who didn't have the patience to wait up for the sick child falling behind, but with myself, the little boy who desperately wanted to be normal rather than pitied and forgotten.

I was fragile.

After the transplant, it took months to recover. I struggled to put even a little bit of weight on. I was constantly visiting doctors, constantly getting blood tests. I'm grateful for the second chance I've had at life—God knows that other children have not been so lucky. But in those many months of recovery, not to mention the months before the transplant, one message was on a continuous loop in my mind:

Be careful. You are fragile.

This was the constant refrain I received from my doctors and my mother: *You are too fragile to play football, or basketball, or baseball. You must take care of your health and protect your kidney.* The message was well intentioned, but it had lasting repercussions. Now, as I near fifty years old, I *still* live my life as though I'm too fragile.

It's true that playing sports causes me physical pain. But how much of that pain is really mental? How much of it is my brain searching my body for proof of my fragility? This is the constant dance my brain and body go through: the brain seeking pain and the body providing it, all to confirm my fragility. My mind *craves* the pain as proof that I am fragile.

After years of being told I was fragile, I ended up fragile. I didn't intend for that to happen. I lived life not noticing the devil on my shoulder constantly whispering, "I am fragile," informing each decision. I was just being. I wasn't aware of what I was doing. I certainly wasn't aware of why I was doing it.

But then, a few years ago, with a lot of meditation and journaling, I realized what had been holding me back: *me*. My brain played this constant loop of "I am fragile" in the background of my life that kept me from taking even small, calculated risks. I stayed comfortable. I stayed close to safety. If I were a ship's captain, my boat would have never truly gone out to sea; I always stayed within reach of the shore.

And there is nothing wrong with that—until there is. Until you wake up one day wanting more than the comfortable life you put yourself in. Until you wake up and say, I never did this thing... and I regret it.

I hope to wake you up to that desire so you're not on your deathbed regretting not doing whatever it is you want to do. I hope to bring awareness to whatever it is you tell yourself you can't do, so you can be mindful of how you keep yourself safe through the story you tell yourself.

For some of us—including me—that story is influenced by racism, which affects how we view ourselves. We may wonder whether we deserve our goals and dreams. We may subconsciously tell ourselves we don't deserve more because of what society has told us about ourselves for centuries.

For me, it's similar to reminding myself of my fragility and making decisions based on that mindset. We often make decisions based on what we have been told about our Blackness all of our lives; but even worse, we have been told this for generations. The negative messaging is ingrained in our DNA. We unconsciously make decisions based on that messaging.

We must be aware of the decisions we make and why we make them. When we are mindful of why we do things, it makes it easier to choose differently. Once I gained awareness about how I viewed my fragility, I was able to look at my decision-making differently. I'd ask, Is my decision to do this borne from my belief that I am fragile? What other decisions can I make? Does making a different decision lead to other opportunities?

And then the work gets fun: *Does this other decision get me closer to the person I truly want to be? Does this decision get me closer to the best version of myself? Is doing this other thing what my soul wants to do?*

That is why being conscious of the decisions we make is so important. When we start with the premise that our decisions have gotten us to where we sit today, we have the ability to move our lives in a different direction. It gives us license. It gives us control. It gives us power.

> WHEN WE START WITH THE PREMISE THAT OUR DECISIONS HAVE GOTTEN US TO WHERE WE SIT TODAY, WE HAVE THE ABILITY TO MOVE OUR LIVES IN A DIFFERENT DIRECTION.

The Privilege Race

There is a famous video discussing race and privilege where college-aged kids line up in a race to win a hundred dollars.[3] However, before the race begins, the race starter allows a head start for the runners based on their circumstances. The racers get to take two steps forward if any of the following applies to them:

- Parents who are still married to each other

- A father figure in the home

- Access to private education

- Access to a free tutor

- Never having to worry about the cell phone being shut off

- Not having to help Mom or Dad pay household bills

- Not having to pay for college

- Never having to wonder where the next meal is coming from

As each statement is read, those to whom it applies move forward two steps. When the speaker is finished, everyone is asked to look around. They notice that all the kids in front with the biggest head start are white, and the ones furthest behind are Black.

Two things strike me about this experience. First, the statements in the list have nothing to do with decisions the participants did or didn't make but rather are due to decisions their *parents* made. Second, *racial identity is not on the list.*

Father figures aren't exclusive to white homes. It's not a "white thing" to not have to worry about your next meal.

The privileges these participants enjoyed were the results of someone's decisions, not their race. Just as it's not a child's fault they were born into a home that could not afford private school, it is also not the child's fault they have two parents in the home. Neither of those individuals were in control of their circumstances. Their privilege was a result of decisions their parents made, not their race.

This race for a hundred dollars parallels life in American society with many of us having an advantage—privilege— and starting far ahead of our peers upon leaving home as young adults. It's not our peer's fault he was born into a home that could not afford a private school education. It is also not the "privileged" person's fault that she had two parents in the home. Neither of those circumstances were in the young adults' control.

Though they might be unfamiliar to us, these circumstances are real, especially for the child who is wondering about their next meal. But is that the result of privilege? Or is that the result of the parents' decision-making?

If we want our children to take sixteen steps forward in the privilege race, we can start making decisions today—even if we do not have children—to get them that head start.

Drawing Out the Life You Want

It's important to draw out the life you want, or else you may end up just living the life that you have around you. Having grown up in the suburbs of Chicago, I find myself living in a very similar suburb because I consciously and subconsciously recreated the environment I knew. For the most part, my own life is a re-creation of what I saw growing up. I am not special. I am just doing what I saw around me. I was lucky to have the resources I needed to become a lawyer and create the life I live. And while I am aware that many do not have those same resources, there is always a path forward. Part of that is surrounding yourself with people who are doing what you want to be doing. If you want to be a doctor, you need to hang around doctors. If you want to be a lawyer, hang around lawyers. If you want to be a millionaire, hang around millionaires. If you want to be a churchgoer, you'll need to hang out with other churchgoers. You are the average of the five people closest to you.[4]

> IT'S IMPORTANT TO DRAW OUT THE LIFE YOU WANT, OR ELSE YOU MAY END UP JUST LIVING THE LIFE THAT YOU HAVE AROUND YOU.

When you drive to an unfamiliar place, you need to map out how you get there—and the same concept applies to where you are going in life. Just like people will give you directions to the mall, people will help direct you to where you want to be in life. When someone asks to sit down with me for a coffee because they want to become a lawyer and need directions to get there, I gladly find time.

But know that once you have the directions, you need to do the work. Just like you need to follow directions to get to the mall, you need to follow directions and do the work to get to wherever you are going in life.

However, before you can even ask directions, you must know where you're trying to go. Imagine what you want your life to look like. Have fun with it. And don't settle for small—instead, allow yourself to think big and be creative. Take a moment and write your intended destination. Keep that journal entry with you; you may choose to use it as a bookmark as you read.

Now that you have your destination in mind, keep this with you. Look at it regularly. *Feel* that lifestyle—what it's like to live in your dream house, in your dream part of the world, comfortable in your finances. Start being the person you want to be in five years. Start owning your future.

You may not yet own the security or education or house or vacation home or financial portfolio or family life you want, but if you are confident that it's possible, you'll do the work to get it. You will, consciously and subconsciously, make decisions to put yourself into a position to make that a reality. Your life will be about taking small, continuous steps toward that destination.

Sometimes the realization hits me that I am not being the man I want to be. It's okay to feel this way. That's why the goals you write down are so important—because you may have to find your way *back* to who you want to be.

Do not beat yourself up about past decisions. The past is the past. A wise client, Anthany Frazier, once told me that by dwelling on yesterday's mistake, we lose the game today. We all make mistakes, and we should use those mistakes to evaluate the decisions that got us where we currently are. But then we need to get back to work on our dreams.

I recently went to a party with friends I have known for decades but hadn't seen in a while. It was great to catch up, but I noticed they had all gained a couple of extra pounds that come with age.

Then I looked at myself in the mirror and saw the weight that had crept onto my own body. As I considered my past decisions, I noticed a pattern: working out less, less cardio, no walks, eating a little too much, snacking after 9:00 p.m. in front of the television. One recent Friday night included skipping dinner, having two too many drinks with salted peanuts and Cheez-Its, and then eating *an entire frozen pizza* while on my back as I rewatched *Narcos* at one in the morning. Although I'm not a dietician, I assume that wasn't good for my midsection.

That growing belly—that weight creep—was a consequence of my decision-making.

If your goal is to get in shape, you must first define "getting in shape." Do you have a specific weight goal? Would you like to run a 5K, or run a 5K in a certain time? Is it walking around your block? Whatever it is, take that one little step to move you closer to that goal—and don't forget to celebrate your wins. Your subconscious will thank you for it.

This same principle—one step at a time—applies to any other goal you want to meet. For example, let's say your goal is to become a millionaire, and you've taken these steps:

- You've sought out the wealthiest person you know for insight into how they got to where they are.

- You've bought the books *The Millionaire Next Door* by Thomas J. Stanley and *Think and Grow Rich* by Napoleon Hill and keep them on your nightstand.

- You've evaluated your spending to trim the fat in your budget.

- You've created a savings plan.

- You are figuring out how to invest in yourself to create

more income—by finding a new job, going back to school, or creating a side hustle.

You're well on your way to allowing your decisions to impact your future and where you want to go. Here are some other steps you can take to move you toward your goal:

Work out. Working out regularly may not directly impact your bottom line, but it does change your mindset, making it easier to move forward in your journey. If you work out regularly, you see and feel the effects of sticking to a system and a plan. You see your body transform, and you notice you have greater endurance. Those changes build confidence. If you keep your promise to work out, you will tend to keep other promises you've made to yourself. You are much more likely to continue investing in yourself if you are already investing in your health.

Read regularly. Whether it's becoming a millionaire or achieving some other goal, you can invest in yourself by reading books. Studies show that the mental stimulation from reading a book decreases the risk of Alzheimer's disease and dementia.[5] In the same way that working out helps the muscles of the body, reading helps the brain. A 2009 University of Sussex study found reading reduces stress.[6] Everyday life is hard, and reading can often allow us to escape those challenges for a moment.

Connect to an accountability partner. We often have people we gossip or complain with. Find someone you can *grow* with.

Find a mentor. With whatever goal you've set, seek out someone you admire whom you can model. In our millionaire example, perhaps you're thinking, *I don't know any millionaires.* That's okay; you don't have to actually know them. One of my mentors, Ed Mylett, doesn't even know I exist. But I read his books, follow him on Instagram, and listen to his podcast on my commute. I spend five hours a week sitting with mentors like Mylett, Lewis Howes, Tony Robbins, and Matthew Bivens (all podcasters I listen to—and the podcasts are free!). You will build momentum by listening to relevant podcasts, watching mentors on YouTube, and reading books that interest you.

Navigating Systemic Racism

When you change the way you look at things,
the things you look at change.
—Dr. Wayne Dyer

Kidney disease is a big part of my story and a big reason I am so concerned with staying safe. Being a kidney transplant patient became a part of me, a part of my mindset and my everyday being. Can I participate in an activity without endangering my kidney and my health? Every decision I made ran through that calculation—and over years and decades of viewing life like that—*am I able to do this?*—I subconsciously limited myself.

Does systemic racism have a similar impact? Do we think we deserve to see our dreams come true, or are we subconsciously thinking we don't because of what society has told Black people about ourselves for centuries? Having been repeated over generations, is this negative messaging ingrained in our DNA?

Racism may have played a role in where you are right now. Perhaps it plays a role in the options you have and the decisions you've made. Racism can influence our tendency to make decisions that lead to more destructive results— because those destructive choices are easier and more available. Perhaps that is one way to look at racism. If we accept that our decisions put us in the position we are in and that racism gives Black and brown people poorer options, making it easier to make destructive decisions, then maybe we defeat racism by making different decisions. And making different decisions can lead to better options.

We are often seen as more dangerous because of the way we have been depicted for centuries. We have been depicted as less intelligent as whites. Barack Obama went to Harvard Law School and was the president of the *Harvard Law Review,* yet when Newt Gingrich called this merely a product of affirmative action, some white people nodded their heads in agreement. That's just one example of why we often have to work harder than whites to get into similar positions.

The collective subconscious of Americans—across the racial spectrum—reduces the value of Black lives. A Black woman falling asleep in a Yale dorm? She doesn't belong here—call the police. A Black man jogging in a neighborhood in Georgia who doesn't belong? Three white men feel entitled to shoot him to death. A Black child in Cleveland carrying a toy gun? The police yell "Stop, police!" and then wait less than two seconds and shoot to kill.

That's why purses shift when I get on an elevator. That's why doors lock when I walk through a parking lot at a supermarket. That's why car dealers will give me worse financing or deals than a white man with the same wealth, credit, and income on the same car. It is not done consciously. This bias was caused by centuries of stories American society has told about Black Americans.

That's why an approach that puts the focus on what *we can do* takes the power away from the collective subconscious of a nation of 350 million. The focus is not on what we can do to defeat racism; the focus is on what we can do to defeat the *effects* of racism. That approach puts the onus on us rather than society. We can't force a nation of 350 million people to change its collective subconscious. But *I* can change. *We* can change. I'm not saying that society is perfect, that there isn't racism, and we shouldn't try to change it. I am saying that if we wait for society to change, generation after generation will continue to fall victim to racism and its effects. By acknowledging racism and making conscious decisions in spite of it, we can eradicate it from another angle. When we consciously make decisions to build the lives we want, rather than reacting to the lives we have, we'll create better options not only for us but for our children and their children.

Changing the prism to think that way is an issue that transcends race. Plenty of people merely react to circumstances rather than consciously making intentional decisions based on where they want to be in five years, regardless of race.

THE FOCUS IS ON WHAT WE CAN DO TO DEFEAT THE *EFFECTS* OF RACISM

The takeaway is not that Black people make poor decisions because of racism. It's that *everyone* makes poor decisions. *Everyone* reacts to their emotions. However, because of racism, Black people have more generational self-image issues and societal hurdles to overcome when we do react and make a poor decision.

Being conscious of the decisions we make is the first step. It puts us back in control of our fate. We are in control.

Not the system. Not "the man." If racism affects the consequences of our decisions, if racism amplifies poor decisions, can we collectively decide to focus on making better decisions, giving us less opportunity to be affected by racism?

If a Black man and a white man both get caught using cocaine, is it more likely that the Black man will receive a stiffer sentence? Absolutely. Is that fair? Absolutely not. We can and should continue to bring light to such inequity. But *if we decide not to use cocaine in the first place*, we can also render that inequity irrelevant for us as individuals.

Racism is a bit like gravity: No matter what we do, it's always there. But even gravity can be overcome by airplanes and rockets. We do ourselves a favor by acknowledging that racism exists and then banding together to make better individual decisions that in turn lead to better collective options.

The fact is that Black people can create an *awesome* existence within American society. Despite its problems, this is still the land of opportunity. Examples abound of Black millionaires and billionaires who made their fortunes off their talents. Should there be more? Can you be one? Absolutely. But to do it, you need to decide to do it.

Life is not fair. The world may not be fair to you because of your skin color. But it's also not fair to the person whose child is fighting cancer, or to the person who gets hit by a drunk driver and spends the rest of their life in a wheelchair. It's not fair to the person minding their business who gets shot in gang crossfire. It's not fair for people who are born with medical or mental disabilities that make the world markedly more difficult for them to navigate.

WE DO OURSELVES A FAVOR BY ACKNOWLEDGING THAT RACISM EXISTS AND THEN BANDING TOGETHER TO MAKE BETTER INDIVIDUAL DECISIONS THAT IN TURN LEAD TO BETTER COLLECTIVE OPTIONS.

Life was not fair to me. I didn't choose to be born with a single failing kidney that required a lifesaving surgery at thirteen and again at thirty-two. I didn't choose to have my growth stunted due to the disease or to take a dozen pills daily to keep my immune system from attacking a foreign organ in my body. But I did have the choice between sitting back and being sad about my circumstances and figuring how to live my best life while taking lifesaving medication.

Lamar Jackson, quarterback for the Baltimore Ravens, has a T-shirt that says "Nobody cares. Work harder." That's an effective mindset to have, though it's not entirely true. People *do* care when they consciously consider the inequities that abound in America. Unfortunately, it's the subconscious decisions Americans make about people of color that persist over generations. That said, my opportunities are much better than the opportunities my parents, aunts, and uncles had just one generation ago. In my lifetime, America has provided me more opportunity than my white mother's family growing up in the 1960s.

Though I was raised with privilege, my parents were not. Even my white mother did not have the same privileges I've enjoyed, which were the direct result of decisions my parents made. Merriam-Webster defines *privilege* as a "right or immunity attached specifically to a position or an office." Privilege is also defined as "to accord a higher value or superior position to."[7] Privilege can be earned. Privilege comes from doing little things repeatedly to get you toward your goal. Because my parents did little things over and over again decades ago, my privilege grew, and my children live in privilege today.

To get to "privilege," I ask that you change the prism in which we view racism. The prism you view the world in today is 100 percent correct. It's *your prism*. My prism is also 100 percent correct—it's my prism. But if we want different results, we need to do different things. To make it easier to do different things, perhaps we should start by changing the prism in which we view our lives.

CHAPTER THREE

Looking through Our Own Prism

I REMEMBER . . .

I remember a youngish Black man making a speech about the purple states of America in 2004.

I remember voting for that man and being in Grant Park when he won the presidency in 2008.

I remember holding my firstborn one month later, in a hospital less than two miles from Grant Park.

I remember feeling dread seeing the president of the United States hung in effigy by "patriots."

I remember feeling as though I was under attack by these people because of my skin color.

I remember feeling under attack when we spoke up about racial inequity in policing.

I remember when a man's right to take a knee during the national anthem was attacked.

I remember Black Lives Matter being called a terrorist organization.

I remember being quarantined during a global pandemic feeling utterly helpless as cities were looted in response to yet another death of an unarmed Black man at the hands of the police.

I remember feeling anger toward white people.

I remember sitting on my back patio and crying because of that anger, because of that helplessness, because of that hopelessness for my home, my friends, and my country.

Because of George Floyd.

Because of Tamir Rice.

Because of Eric Garner.

Because of Abner Louima.

Because, as a Black man in America, I *am* them.

I am a Black man in America. We live in a society that views us as Black first and foremost. We live in a society that equates Blackness to dangerousness. People call the police when they are in danger—which means they call the police on Black people in white spaces. The Black person, solely because of their Blackness, does not belong. Our Blackness puts the white person in fear. What did Lolade Siyonbola do wrong when she fell asleep in a Yale dormitory's common area? She could not have said or done anything intimidating because she was asleep. She didn't assault anyone while asleep. It was only her Blackness that somehow put a white person in such imminent fear that they had to call the police.

Having the police called on our Blackness is an epidemic. White people use our Blackness against us when they misbehave: "If you don't stop questioning what I'm doing, I'll call the police and tell them you're harassing me." A woman named Amy Cooper called the police on a Black man named Christian Cooper. In her emergency call she claimed a Black man was harassing her. Those type of calls lead to encounters between police officers and Black men that can end up tragic for the Black men involved.

My being a Black man means I am dangerous. My being a Black man does not mean Father. My being a Black man does not mean Husband. My being a Black man does not mean Business Owner. My being a Black man does not mean

Author. My being a Black man does not mean Lawyer or Employer.

We live in an America where because of my Blackness, I need to make white people feel comfortable with my being in "their" space. In their dorm common areas. In their Starbucks coffee shop. In their public swimming pool. In their public park. In their public street while jogging. In their neighborhoods when I drive through them. In their public golf courses. We have to make them feel comfortable when we've earned enough money to drive nice cars.

Because as a Black man, my Blackness makes me a little less equal than all (white) men that are created equal.

When I was in preschool, we lived in a tiny two-bedroom apartment in Addison, Illinois. It was 1977. I don't have memories of places I lived before that, although I'm told there were a few. I went to this preschool—daycare—while my parents worked to pay rent and put food on the table. I don't know if we were poor. I know that my father worked for the phone company, Illinois Bell, as a lineman. He got up on telephone poles and fixed lines in the 1970s. Back then, Illinois Bell used three-foot wooden spools—like a giant spool of thread—to spool the wire that went between the phone company and our homes and businesses. My family used those large wooden spools as furniture.

I don't remember my parents taking me to and from

school, nor do I remember the school. However, I do recall one of my four-year-old classmates telling me that my father was *Black* and my mother was white. Up until then, I had not noticed. They were Mom and Dad to me, not my "white mother" and "black father." It's been said that people don't remember what you say but rather how you make them feel. This is my first example of remembering how I felt, as this little four-year-old boy made me feel inadequate. Because my father is Black, he was less than; because he is my father, I am less than. And this was from a four-year-old white boy—where did he learn that? From his parents? From our teacher?

In 1981, in third grade, I was on the playground during recess at Jackson School in Elmhurst, Illinois. As I ran around with my friends, two fourth graders, Bill and Tim, hurled *nigger* at me. Several times. I remember this specifically; I certainly remember how it made me feel: less than. These boys were better than me because of my skin color. My Blackness made me less than. My Blackness made me inferior. My Blackness made me subhuman. I remember being alone. I remember crying.

I did not know what the word *nigger* meant. I had certainly heard it before, very likely in my vicinity, but it hadn't cut me the same way as it did on the Jackson School playground.

I asked my white mother what *nigger* meant. Stale

cigarette smoke hung in the tiny kitchen as she held me close on a small kitchen chair that had duct tape covering the tears in the vinyl. I was that chair. Cut open by language we've heard for centuries. Cut open by language as prevalent in American culture as apple pie. Like with the small vinyl chair before me, my mother took out her duct tape to cover my cuts, my wounds. She sat there, with tears in her eyes, taping the damage that America had done to a completely innocent eight-year-old. The world had told her child that his Blackness made him insignificant. The irony lost on her son was that he went to the person who looked like the fourth graders to explain what they meant.

On that day, my mother told me the word says more about the people using it than it does about the person it is directed to. That *nigger* is an ugly word, and the people using that term are the real niggers. They, not me, are the ugly ones.

Her response may have made it easier for me to ignore or dodge the pain I felt when I heard the word in the future or was otherwise reminded of the fact that as a Black man in America, I am inferior, but it didn't change that our society puts a premium on race: White is the pinnacle of beauty. Black is dangerous.

We can debate the validity of my mother's construct, but for me it created a matrix where the people who used *nigger* and looked at race first are the ugly ones, rather than me and my race. It created a reality where race is a component of what makes me, but not *the* component. Race is still a struggle for me in our society—even forty years later—because I understand that my Blackness always precedes Brian Thomas into rooms. But my mother created the construct that I *belonged* in the room and that questioning my being in the room was on them, not me. It was that experience in my mother's arms that built the prism through which I viewed life.

Your Prism Dictates Your Actions

In his 2015 book *Between the World and Me*, Ta-Nehisi Coates shares the story of his young son being pushed by a white woman as they left a theater. The woman said nothing but "Come on!" to the young boy, who was dawdling as a five-year-old does. Coates interprets this event as racist: a white woman is assuming that she has the authority to control a Black body. Reacting to his young son being touched, Coates's anger swelled and he called the woman out.

His interpretation may have been correct. His interpretation may have been wrong. The easiest interpretation (admittedly from my prism) is the woman was just rude. Maybe the woman had a leaky bladder and had to get to the restroom. Maybe the woman found out her child was in the emergency room and she had to get there as soon as possible; maybe she wasn't thinking about the color of the body in her way but rather viewed it as an impediment to where she had to be. There are hundreds of possible interpretations for why the woman did what she did. Coates viewed it as a racist act because of the prism through which he views life.

But the woman's actual intent doesn't matter. Like Coates, we infer intent. When a car cuts us off on the highway, we'll never know the intent. The driver is long gone and we are left stewing in their wake. We sit in anger, while the driver moves on, not thinking of us one bit. Then we take that anger to the office with us. We're curt with our coworkers; we inadvertently bump someone as we get off an elevator, all because of how we viewed an event taking place in our recent past. We don't even realize we're doing it. Ironically, if the person we inadvertently bump in an angered rush off the elevator stereotypes Black people as "rude," now, we've provided proof their stereotype of Blacks must be correct.

Coates's experience ended with a white man coming to the defense of the white woman; a gentlemanly attempt to coax "the beast" (Coates's words) into submission. Coates eventually let the moment pass, but did so because he realized his son stood there witnessing the event. The event clearly branded itself into Coates's memory. But what if he inferred a racist intent that was never there to begin with? It's possible that Coates is carrying this anger just because a white woman had a leaky bladder.

That is what we do. We take these stories—the same way I was able to recount the story of my mother telling me that the person using the word *nigger* was actually the nigger—and put them in our mental backpack and carry them around with us the rest of our lives. Many of these stories are negative—reasons why we can't do something. The stories we tell ourselves are mental limitations on what we cannot do and why we cannot do it. Even worse, many of these stories are false. Coates's belief that a white woman is a racist reinforces the prism in which he views life: that the people who call themselves white always seek to assert dominance over Black people.

We'll never know whether Coates's interpretation of events that happened to him ten years ago is correct. Yet these stories—the statements we tell ourselves—are examples of the prisms through which we view life. By shining a light on these stories, we can examine whether we are driving outcomes based on our prism. And if so, can we change our outcomes by changing our view through the prism?

Have you ever gone car shopping, decided on a car you like, and then suddenly seen it all over the place? That particular make and model is in your consciousness and your focus is directed on it. It's likely that the car is no more present today than it was a year ago, but you haven't noticed it because you haven't been looking for it.

Our brains provide for this. People smarter than me call this the Reticular Activating System (RAS).[8] As German designer, entrepreneur, and Renaissance man Tobias van Schneider explained:

> Your RAS takes what you focus on and creates a filter for it. It then sifts through data and presents only the pieces that are important to you. All of this happens without you noticing, of course. The RAS programs itself to work in your favor without you actively doing anything. Pretty awesome, right?

> In the same way, the RAS seeks information that validates your beliefs. It filters the world through the parameters you give it, and your beliefs shape those parameters. If you think you are bad at giving speeches, you probably will be. If you believe you work efficiently, you most likely do. The RAS helps you see what you want to see and in doing so, influences your actions.[9]

That is why the prism we see life through is so important. The actual story we tell ourselves, the prism in which we view life, is more important than the events that happen to us. We will interpret the events through that prism, through that story. If we view life through the prism of race being a prominent part of our lives, we will find examples of that daily. Our brain will find them. It could be as simple as a white woman moving our slow-moving toddler out of her way. Should she have put her hand on him? No. But Coates left that encounter believing it to be an example of racist behavior when it easily could have been that the lady had to go to the bathroom really, really bad.

I once worked out with a trainer who gave me a weighted vest. I had to put on the twenty-five-pound vest and climb up and down a hill. It was a tough workout! The cooldown was taking the vest off and climbing the hill—which was a cinch by comparison.

Now imagine that weighted vest being a mental backpack where we keep many experiences that solidify the way we view the world. What I'm asking is that we take the backpack off, open it up, sift through it, and take the things out that aren't serving us. When we joke about another person's baggage, this is literally what we're talking about. Valid memories of what happened to us twenty years ago may serve us today; but memories layered with our interpretation of an event—a woman pushing our son out of the way because she is a racist—may not.

To seek the future you want, take off your mental back-pack. Do you have beliefs that do not serve you to get where you want to go? Do you carry beliefs that make it more difficult to reach your life goals? We can choose to interpret our experiences to result in better outcomes. Is race a construct that we need to be aware of? Most definitely. But it is not *the* construct. Most of the time, race will not prevent you from living the life you want unless you allow it to. Shift your prism slightly, and perhaps you can change your outcomes.

CHAPTER FOUR

Change the Prism through Which You View the World

I PLAYED WITH kaleidoscopes as a child. Remember those? They were tubes that you looked through and when you twisted the tube, a different beautiful and bright mosaic appeared in the lens. For those of you who have never played with one, I offer you Wikipedia's definition:

> A kaleidoscope (/kəˈlaɪdəskoʊp/) is an optical instrument with two or more reflecting surfaces (or mirrors) tilted to each other at an angle, so that one or more (parts of) objects on one end of these mirrors are shown as a regular symmetrical pattern when viewed from the other end, due to repeated reflection. These reflectors are usually enclosed in a tube, often containing on one end a cell with loose, colored pieces of glass or other transparent (and/or opaque) materials to be reflected into the viewed pattern. *Rotation*

*of the cell causes motion of the materials, resulting in
an ever-changing view being presented.*[10]

The last line of the definition moves me: *rotation of the cell
causes motion of the materials, resulting in an ever-changing view
being presented.* Isn't that life? We are born. We experience the
world and learn from those experiences. As we experience and
learn, the cell rotates, *resulting in an ever-changing view being
presented.* As our parents teach us lessons—by what they say
and what they do—the cell rotates, *resulting in an ever-changing
view being presented.* We find ourselves with friends and peers
who share lessons and experiences and the cell rotates, *resulting
in an ever-changing view being presented.* Those friend groups
shift over time—from work peers, school peers, kids' friends'
parents, neighbors—and each group, each person provides a
slightly different view of the world, causing the cell to rotate,
resulting in an ever-changing view being presented.

We must admit that our experience of this world changed
significantly from when we were five years old to thirteen.
And again to twenty. Isn't that true at fifty? Or sixty? Why is
it we feel like we know everything there is to know at twenty-
five and don't allow the kaleidoscope to rotate anymore? Can
rotating the kaleidoscope enhance our life experience?

I want to awaken you to the matrix that we're in. It's one
of our own creation based on the way we view the world.

We spend time arguing and fighting about our identities—be it political, religious, racial, national, even sports teams—which are borne from the randomness of our birth. Our identities are based on the happenstance of where we were born and to whom we were born. We had no control about the country and community we were born within. Yet we judge people for these things. I cringe at the notion of a racist hating me for the color of my skin—something I have no control over. Why not hate me for something I control? For the person I am? For the content of my character? Or choose to love me for it, regardless of my Blackness?

YOU CONTROL THE WAY YOU VIEW LIFE.

You control the way you view life. You control what you create in this life. Our subconscious creates the matrix—which keeps us asleep to our control of our lives when we react to stimuli. We allow our subconscious to make our decisions for us and react to stimuli, just like Pavlov's dog. Just writing that phrase—"like Pavlov's dog"—caused me to think about George Clinton's *Atomic Dog* and my head started nodding to the beat. (Are you doing it now?) This ironically illustrates my point: our brains are wired in such a way that a years-old thought or experience will cause the same reaction when we encounter the same stimulus. Think about the smell of a bakery or a cookie Grandma made when you were a child and how your brain can instantly transport you back to that time and place.

If you view life as one where racism will always keep Black and brown people subservient to whites, then that is the lens through which you view life. If you view life as a picture of Black and brown lives being systemically subjugated to those of the white man, when you find an example of it in everyday life—which will happen—just like Pavlov's dog, you will nod your head to the picture you've created within the kaleidoscope.

That is a totally valid picture. You can view life that way and find examples of it.

But does that life view get you where you want to be?

If it doesn't, then consider changing the cells of the kaleidoscope and maybe you'll view life differently. Change the prism to put you in the driver's seat of your life. Change the prism so you are a thoughtful creator rather than a person who reacts to a stimulus and then lives a life that was built on those reactions. It is easy to be divorced and unemployed when you react to a stimulus as it comes in. Reacting to your boss the wrong way can get you fired; reacting to another man or woman can get you divorced. Reacting to that asshole can get you charged. Reacting to the police can get you killed.

As I've said before, if you don't know where you're going, you can end up anywhere. Whereas by knowing where you want to go in life, by drawing out the picture and making decisions to take you toward a goal, you can create the life you want to live. And in creating that life—by moving toward that end—you become a different person. You become a person that manifests things. That manifests that home. That manifest that education. That manifests that bank account.

When you want to manifest things, you start seeing opportunities. And those opportunities can cause you to change the prism though which you view life.

This doesn't mean we won't still be affected by racism. Racism won't magically disappear from our life. But the effects of racism will change. Racism won't be an unclimbable wall, but rather a hurdle. Something we shouldn't have to encounter but can get over with some additional effort.

My great fortune was that my parents did all the hard work. They decided to do things differently from what their parents and families modeled. They put me on a path filled with opportunities. They put me on a path with privilege.

Growing up in my home, I know that my privilege was earned. My parents made decisions. They decided to remain married and to provide their children the opportunity to get college educations. They decided to move to a location where college was the norm. They decided to work hard in their jobs, creating wealth but more importantly modeling a work ethic while showing the rewards of hard work. Were we vacationing in Italy? Hell no. But I had everything I needed. And everything I needed put me in position to vacation with my children in Italy today.

I am fortunate that my parents viewed life through the "hard work pays dividends" lens. That's the way they viewed the kaleidoscope. Having a Black father and white mother in the '80s, when people pointed at us as we *drove in a car together as a family*, taught us to thumb our noses at what others thought. Instead, we thought, *We'll do us. We'll work hard and show them.*

Did racism affect me? Absolutely. But I will not allow racism to affect where I want to go. Racism does not affect my dreams and my desire and my work ethic. Like gravity, racism is something that will be until the end of my days on this planet. What muscles do I need to build to defy gravity? If I want to jump higher, what muscles do I need to strengthen?

Building these mental muscles affects us individually—which over time may affect racism collectively. Yes, racism affects me; however, because of the privilege I have been afforded by my parents' (and my) decision-making, I have more choices to defeat the effect of most racist acts.

My hope is that if we all build ourselves and our children (and their children) this privilege, that collective build can get our country to a point where the effects of racism are minimized.

We are not going to be able to change peoples' hearts overnight. But I do think that over time peoples' hearts have changed. The country views segregation today a lot differently than it did in 1945. Racism and racist acts are viewed differently today than they were in 1975.

But it still exists. Rather than relying on America's heart to change *today*, let's rely on *ourselves* to change. I can't control my neighbor. I can't control my friend. How am I going to control some stranger before an encounter we share? But I can control myself. I can control my reaction to getting pulled over for driving while Black.

I can control my decision-making. I can control building muscles so I can jump higher. I choose to work on me. I choose to set goals. I choose to intentionally create the life I want.

And you know what? Some days when you're building muscles, you suffer a tear or injury. Or you need rest. Take a break. Smile and have fun. But after a day or two or a week's vacation, get back to work on you.

Will racism continue to affect me? Yes and no. Yes, people will react—consciously or subconsciously—to my Blackness. No, because my focus is on not allowing their reaction to my Blackness to affect my goals.

And that is the prism through which I see racism.

Some people choose to live their lives looking through a different prism, for instance: "As a Black woman, race has always been a prominent part of my life. I have never been able to escape the fact that I am a Black woman in a white supremacist country."[11] And that is 100 percent correct. That view is 100 percent valid. That is their prism. It is their life. It is their choice to live life that way.

At times, I lived life that way. I carried my Blackness with me in every room I walked, examining others' reactions to me, feeling for an energy shift in the room because of my presence, and looking for other Black faces so I could feel more comfortable. And then I didn't. I chose not to. And my life became a little easier. That mental backpack became lighter. I stopped carrying the "Do I belong here?" question around with me most places I went. This world can be so difficult—consider how much more difficult we make it on ourselves when our prism is constantly assessing whether our Blackness precludes us from being in a room. We limit ourselves by constantly calculating our value *everywhere*. We do this in the workplace, in an interview, in a bank, in a car dealership, in a nice hotel on vacation. Think about all of that wasted energy that could be put to better use.

Just like in a kaleidoscope, changing your prism ever so slightly will change your entire view.

When we acknowledge that we see life through the prism we were conditioned to see it through (by family, friends, and society), we can choose to adjust the prism and see how life looks. And if we don't like how life looks within that prism, we can choose to shift it again. And again and again, until we find a view we like for that particular season of our life.

Because of your conditioning, you may need your current view. That's fine. But look at it. Examine why you need that view. Maybe through that examination, you'll learn why you look at life that way. And when you understand your why, you may learn that you can shift a belief ever so slightly and live a life *you* want to live rather than the life you were programmed to live.

Say to yourself, I'll start doing things I want to do without considering my skin color, without considering the *I can't do that because of how society views me* mindset. Do things you want to do for a day or a week or two weeks and see how things work. Empower yourself to figure out what you want regardless of your skin color. Empower yourself to figure out what you want regardless of your body type. Empower yourself to figure out what you want regardless of your sex or sexuality or gender or where you live or your socioeconomic background or your education level or your perceived intel-ligence or your past or whatever excuse you tell yourself for why you can't do what you want to do.

Empower yourself to figure out what you want. And then empower yourself to go for it! Make a plan to get to that goal. Find someone who has achieved that goal and enlist their help. When you surround yourself with these people, you'll find it easier to keep moving forward. Give yourself credit for all the tiny steps you make toward that goal.

That initial decision to take that step—to start the process and ask yourself these questions—will have consequences on your life. You will shift your being from reacting to stimuli to making decisions in order to intentionally create the life you want.

Once you create the goal, you can look at what you do day in and day out and ask yourself, Do my habits reflect my goals? And then start building habits that reflect that goal.

It is not an all-or-nothing approach. One habit you have could be watching television every night between 7 and 10 p.m. to decompress after a long day at work. Maybe you change that habit to twice a week, or watch television from 8 to 10 p.m. so you can work on your side hustle between 7 and 8. Build from there. Build momentum and acknowledge your wins. And accept that you will fall short. When you do, get back up and start over. Or try again. That's why I keep the quotation "Do your habits reflect your goals" framed in my office—to remind myself when I get off course. I can choose to get mad at myself when I do get off course (which I do) or I can remind myself that it's okay to be distracted as long as I come back to it.

Are You Being Enough YOU?

The life I have been very fortunate to live is one that has had a certain amount of privilege. When I started this book, I asked myself if the privilege my parents provided took me out of this conversation. I questioned whether I am Black enough. That question is one I've carried around with me most of my life.

My life consisted of decades of identity crises—from both being "too Black" for some rooms and being "too white" for others. When I started this project, I asked myself—and continue to ask myself as I complete it—whether I am "Black enough" to write it. But that question is bullshit. My life experience and identity can't be pared down to that single question. The question I learned to ask is whether I am being Brian enough. Am I being the person I want to be, in this room, at this time? Am I being the Brian that gets me to future me?

And that's why I decided to put this book and myself out there. I open myself up to ridicule. And it's fine. Two things can come from it: (a) someone sees the example of my parents and sees that a family's socioeconomic trajectory can completely shift in a single generation, and (b) I learn something. I learn things I am unaware of. I learn where I can be better. I don't have all the answers. I don't even know all the questions. But if I can write what I've experienced—which includes watching my parents ascend the socioeconomic ladder, seeing how their decision-making impacted that ascension, acknowledging that their decisions conditioned the way I viewed life, and then waking up to my conditioning to live even more fully—and it helps one person, then I've done what I set out to do. And when I learn something in the process, it turns into a win-win.

With all of that, I leave it to you. This book is less about being a singular road map to privilege, because there are myriad ways to get there. This book is more about shaking you awake, getting you off the autopilot of your conditioning, and letting you know you can get to privilege, whatever that means to you. It is to help you examine the why behind your decisions. I want to recognize centuries of exploitation and display how that abuse affects how we view ourselves. And then ask if that view subconsciously limits what we think we can accomplish. I want you to use your strength to transcend the subconscious limits placed on your expectations by generations of structural racism. To understand that we can live with love and wealth and privilege. My life and the lives of my parents and millions of other Black and brown people proves that.

Give your children the luxury of a foundation that puts them sixteen steps ahead in the privilege race. The farther you move your children forward, the farther you move forward. Test the theory: Is racism keeping me back in the privilege race? Or is my decision-making holding me back? Examining how our decisions impact our privilege provides license to get to privilege—by making different decisions. Once we acknowledge our decisions have impact, we can impact our lives by making different decisions.

CHAPTER FIVE

Let Go of the Victim Mentality

OUR SKIN COLOR has nothing to do with the disadvantages we pass to our children.

Reread that last line.

For centuries, we were less than. We could not vote; we could not get an education; we could not get gainful employment; we could not talk to white people unless spoken to; we could not look at white people; we could not live in areas other than those the system outlined for us to live in. Think about that: we live in a society where everyone is created equal and we're told we're free—we went overseas to fight for that freedom—yet people who are still alive today could not buy a home in a "white" suburb. How is that free?

Today we can do all those things. But we carry the legacy of centuries not being able to live, work, learn, eat, or drink near white people. Racism created boundaries for Black and brown people—for centuries we were told where we could go and, more importantly, where we could not. Race no longer keeps us out of neighborhoods, restaurants, schools, and employment; however, the leash of racism tethered around our necks for centuries still prevents us from leaving the yard.

Look at the following image:

What is your knee-jerk reaction to this photograph? That the horse is stupid for not knowing it can walk away and go where it wants, when it wants? I wonder, does this photograph apply to us as well? The same way I was conditioned to be fragile, have you conditioned yourself to believe something that keeps you tethered in place? Does racism do this to us? Do we unintentionally limit ourselves because of racism—both past and present?

But let's give this photograph some context and perspective. For centuries, our leather leash was a chain. Our ancestors were chained and forced onto slave ships; the ones who survived the journey from Africa were forced into slavery. Black Americans were in bondage longer in the United States than we have been "free." We lived in chains for centuries in the United States. The leash wasn't leather—the leather we dealt with was the whip used on our backs and bodies when we didn't do as the white man said.

The chair you see in the photograph? For centuries that chair was a much larger and weightier anchor: it was the law of the United States that said we were chattel; we were property. We were not people. We could be sold at the whim of the people who owned us. Our master could sell our husbands, wives, or children. Imagine that: you have a master. Your master forces you to work, forces you to live where and how he says to, forces you to eat what he provides. Nothing else. You are unable to go out and get more for yourself. You're not finding a better job. That is your entire miserable existence. You are unable to read because you were not provided an education—and then called ignorant and inferior because you were never taught to read.

White men told us our masters were benevolent, providing us food, shelter, clothing, and discipline that we needed and would not have been able to get otherwise. White men told us slavery was a good thing.

Even the whip was a good thing. For centuries, if we talked back or didn't work fast enough, we got the whip. And if we reached our breaking point and escaped, US law forced our return, and we got the whip even harder to break our courage to ever leave again. The myth of "white benevolence" made white people feel better about the way they treated us.

The only thing Black people had was each other. The only thing we owned was our love for each other. Our love for our family. The love a mother has for her children was something that could not be taken away. That bond between mother and child. That bond between mother and father. The bond between father and son.

Yet our "benevolent" masters could break our bonds of love. Master Thomas loses at poker and needs a couple extra bucks to pay off debts? He'll sell your child like he sells Microsoft stock today. Because that is all we were: *assets for a white man*. Master Thomas is disturbed by your affection for your child—he sells your child to prove a point: that he can. The American legal system provided no rights to Black men and women that contributed much wealth to American whites. You want a better life? It wasn't happening.

Even after slavery was abolished, we were still seen as less than. Over forty years after the Civil War, President Theodore Roosevelt created a scandal of epic proportions by inviting Booker T. Washington to the White House for dinner. In 1901, white people didn't hear "President Roosevelt invites Booker T. Washington for dinner"; they heard "Roosevelt dines with a nigger." A Missouri newspaper even ran a poem on its front page titled "Niggers in the White House."[12] A senator from South Carolina, Benjamin Tillman, said, "The action of President Roosevelt in entertaining that nigger will necessitate our killing a thousand niggers in the South before they will learn their place again."[13]

The chair in the above photo was *not* made of flimsy plastic in 1901. And though the leash may not have been made of chains anymore, it still kept us firmly in place.

Jim Crow and Black Codes

When slavery ended, laws were enacted in many states limiting our freedom. These codes told us where we could work, limited our compensation, and controlled where we could live, how we could live, and how we could travel. They also, through poll taxes or tests, limited our ability to vote. Former Confederate soldiers were police officers and judges who executed and enforced Black Codes, making freeing ourselves from those reins impossible. The birth and rise of the Ku Klux Klan enforced these codes, using intimidation through violence, blood, and death. Klansmen served in the highest levels of government. There was no way to live life free and equal, as our Constitution declared, when white men were authorized, by law, to disenfranchise and kill Black and brown people.

With Black Codes becoming the norm in rural areas of the South, Blacks started moving to cities. As the Black population swelled in Southern cities, Jim Crow laws expanded, creating separate accommodations for Blacks in the South. These laws prevented Blacks from going to restaurants, sleeping in hotels, using public bathrooms, frequenting public pools, or going to the theater. Schools and neighborhoods were segregated. But all those accommodations were inferior to white accommodations. We couldn't even be buried with whites, as cemeteries were segregated.

It was nearly impossible for Black Americans to break into the middle and upper socioeconomic classes due to these restrictions. Entertainers were able to climb the socioeconomic ladder. There is a gut-punch of a scene in the 2020 movie *One Night in Miami* where legendary football player Jim Brown returns to his hometown in 1963 and visits an influential white benefactor (the "benevolent white man"). They have a wonderful conversation on his front porch. The benefactor serves Jim lemonade and treats him as the town hero. They sit there and talk as if they are old friends. As the scene plays on, it seems like the white man is a mentor to Jim Brown. Eventually, the man's adult daughter comes outside and asks her father for help moving a heavy piece of furniture. When Jim offers help, the "benevolent white man" smiles, looks Jim in the eye, and says, "Jim, you know I don't allow niggers into the house." He doesn't deliver the statement with malice, but he doesn't need to, because the malice is in the statement: Niggers, no matter how accomplished and intelligent, are not allowed in white spaces. That's just the way it is.

The GI Bill

World War II broke out and over 1.2 million Black Americans went into the army. We fought in Europe. We fought in Japan. We saw devastating battles; we died and saw our brothers die. In the segregated army, we were treated like second-class citizens. We served in Black units, which caused us to wonder if being in the army made sense for a Black man in 1943. James Thompson, a Black man from Wichita, Kansas, wrote in the *Pittsburgh Courier*:

"*Being an American of dark complexion and some 26 years, these questions flash through my mind: 'Should I sacrifice my life to live half American?' 'Will things be better for the next generation in the peace to follow?'... 'Is the kind of America I know worth defending?'* "[14]

Was it ironic that Black units fought and died in a war against oppression when we lived in a country that sponsored systemic oppression against us? In 1935, the *New York Amsterdam News* argued as much on its editorial pages:

"If the Swastika is an emblem of racial oppression, the Stars and Stripes are equally so. This country has consistently refused to recognize one-tenth of its population as an essential part of humanity... It has systematically encouraged the mass murder of these people through bestial mobs, through denial of economic opportunity, through terrorization." [15]

We fought for freedom with valor, yet when we returned from the fight against tyranny abroad, we encountered tyranny at home. We were denied grants for housing and education within the GI Bill that the "Greatest Generation" was provided. That housing and education led to the Baby Boom and the growth of the "white" suburbs. What white families saw after the war in the 1950s did not apply to our Black families. Our Black families were systemically denied the same prosperity the GI Bill provided. For many, by being denied equal education, we were underemployed. We were denied good housing in communities with resources. We were forced to live in impoverished, under-resourced areas.

By not being uniformly applied, the GI Bill increased

racism and segregation in America. It contributed to the growth of the suburbs, allowing white families to flee away from Black—"white flight"—and grow suburbs that had better housing and better education for white children. Black veterans could not use the benefits of the GI Bill to also move to the suburbs as Jim Crow and redlining, a package of discriminatory practices designed to keep Blacks from buying homes in white neighborhoods, barred these communities even to the few Blacks with the means to move. The freedom we fought and died for overseas was denied to us at home.

Though the GI Bill allowed veterans to obtain a college education or vocational training, Blacks were locked out of these opportunities. For example, some high schools that offered vocational training were in segregated high schools—training that was offered to white veterans was not offered to Black veterans, keeping Black veterans out of the trades. The same was true in universities. Southern colleges and universities barred Black students entirely. Northern universities often put Black admissions applications to the bottom of the pile, effectively keeping us out of their colleges too. Historian Hilary Herbold wrote, "Though Congress granted all soldiers the same benefits theoretically, the segregationist principles of almost every institution of higher learning effectively disbarred a huge proportion of Black veterans from earning a college degree."[16]

Would our society look completely different today had

the GI Bill been applied uniformly to Black veterans and their families? Would there be more Black doctors, lawyers, and CEOs today if we were provided the same educational opportunities seventy years ago that created white doctors, lawyers, and CEOs? We weren't provided those resources. Because our parents and grandparents weren't doctors and lawyers, it limited our opportunity to become doctors and lawyers as well.

The Civil Rights Movement and Beyond

Image from AP

The unequal treatment under the law and the context and irony that America fought for freedoms abroad that were not provided to fellow Americas birthed the civil rights movement.

Firehoses were turned on us and police dogs attacked because we wanted equal rights and opportunities under the law. We had to fight for opportunities granted by the Constitution.

The people who fought for these rights, demonized at the time, are revered today. Today, one of the tragic ironies is that many of the same people and politicians who speak highly of Martin Luther King Jr. demonize the messages of Black Lives Matter and people like Colin Kaepernick who speak about current unequal treatment of Blacks under the law. As much as we have progressed, the age-old battle lines are still drawn.

The constant dog whistles we have heard from politicians and their devotees over the last decade show us that racism is alive and well. President Trump represents millions of Americans who have told us they do not care about our unequal treatment under the law. In response, we can do one of two things: we can wait for white people to care, or we can rely on ourselves.

Change How You Think to Change How You Live

Make no mistake: Black Americans *are* victims. This mentality is generational. We told ourselves for centuries that we are victims. We were victims when our ancestors were forcibly brought here in chains centuries ago; we are still victims when we die at the hand of the police because of our skin color. Being Black in America puts us at a distinct disadvantage. But to move forward, we have to shed that victimhood. Yes, we should acknowledge our history. But then we should acknowledge the present and seek a future that leaves our victimhood behind so we can embody what we share with our ancestors: strength.

Your life is a physical manifestation of the conversation you have in your mind.

Let me repeat that: *Your life is a physical manifestation of the conversation you have in your mind.*

The present tense of victim is survivor, and a future version of surviving is thriving

The present tense of *victim* is *survivor,* and a future version of surviving is thriving. Let's respect yesterday's tragedies by focusing on the fact that we're still fighting. "I am a survivor"—empower yourself with that reminder. Despite all that America has thrown at us, we are still here. There is strength in knowing that we've survived centuries of racism in America. Indeed, the strength of our ancestors courses through our veins.

Once you embrace that truth, you can stop thinking of yourself as a survivor. A survivor is someone pulled from the water after a shipwreck. Surviving shows strength but sits on the doorstep of tragedy. You need to be a victim to be a survivor. You will grow out of the word *survivor* just as you grew out of your shoes when you were seven years old. That word is a stepping stone to get you out of victimhood and into strength.

Your continued existence as a Black person in America is proof that you are strong. Say it five times out loud: *I am strong*. Get that into your head. If life is a physical manifestation of the conversation you are having in your head, when you tell yourself you are strong, your brain will find examples of your strength. Is a department store security guard giving you looks? Remember that you're strong and have every right to be in that department store spending your hard-earned money. We speak our futures into the world, so speak strength.

Effects of Conditioning

I grew up in a predominantly white community. Because of that, I didn't have many opportunities to talk about the effects of racism on my life. It just never came up in conversation as I drank Kool-Aid with the Fischers. The conversations I heard daily were centered on growth-filled futures and creating paths to get there. Like most children, the question I heard most was, "What do you want to be when you grow up?" And when I answered, the adult asking the question took the next step of sitting down and showing me a path to get where I wanted. *You want to be a lawyer? Let's get you in with Julie's dad so he can guide you. You want to be a doctor? Great—you'll sit down with Gregor's dad. You want to be a racecar driver? Awesome, talk to Chris's dad.*

Every day was career day in my neighborhood. Walking into friends' homes provided evidence of possibility. I could become a lawyer because my friends' parents were lawyers; my next-door neighbor was a lawyer. "Lawyer" was not abstract when the guy pulling his trash out on Thursdays was one. Having these resources—and seeing it daily—was incredibly important.

I watched my parents work hard and be rewarded for their hard work. Over roughly ten years, their two beat-up Fords turned into new-model foreign cars. The house became nicer. The drive to St. Louis for a weekend turned into flights to California or Paris. None of that happened by magic. My parents earned every penny. Seeing what my parents earned and accomplished proved that it was possible and fueled and conditioned me to do the same.

My children are also being conditioned. They see hard-working parents. They share a home with a thousand books and see their parents reading them. My children see their parents enjoying the comforts and freedoms associated with the resources that came from that hard work. My children travel. My children live with privilege.

But that privilege doesn't mean we ignore race in our home. My children ask about race and how it affects our lives. My son was pierced by the murder of George Floyd and sought to understand what happened to him and others like him. My daughter moved her first-grade teacher to tears when she told her class that, seventy years ago, she would not have been in the same classroom as her friends because of her race. They have an awareness of race, but it doesn't dominate their lives. Like my wife's left-handedness, it is simply one of the many things that make us who we are.

Though I am cognizant that my Blackness often enters a room before I do, my focus is not on walking through the door but on *what I am in the room to do*. I could dwell on any racism I experience in that room, or on how much harder it was for me than for white folks to be invited in, or on the suspicion that people in the room don't believe I belong because I am Black. Or I can focus on what I came to do, whether that's represent my client, enjoy a meal, purchase a BMW, or anything else. I can't control what other people think about my Blackness, but I *can* control how I feel about it and myself.

That is how I was conditioned and that is how I hope to condition my children.

Resisting the Distraction of Racism

It's often discouraging that society seems to be going backward when it comes to race. A white woman calls the police on a Black birdwatcher in New York's Central Park, claiming he is threatening her when in fact he just asked her to leash her dog.[17] Earlier I mentioned the Black graduate student at Yale who had the police called on her for falling asleep while studying in a dorm's common area. What could be more collegiate than falling asleep in a book while studying? The student, Lolade Siyonbola, was then asked by campus police to prove that she had the right to be there.[18] Would campus police have asked Sara Braasch, the white woman who called the police, to prove her right to be in that dorm? These are just two examples of racist harassment that went viral, but it happens all the time. For example, one of my neighbors will text the neighborhood moms whenever a Black solicitor comes around. (Needless to say, we stopped hanging out with him.) Our neighborhood gets plenty of white solicitors too, but those don't seem to merit text alerts.

Too many white people are conditioned to equate Blackness with danger. One of my neighbors is a Birkenstock-wearing,

Subaru-driving, lived-on-a-commune ultra-liberal, and even she didn't seem fazed when our other neighbor sent out those alert texts. It was only when my wife brought them to her attention that she realized the racism involved. This woman makes my politics look like Ronald Reagan's, and even she didn't "get it" until it was explained to her.

Did Amy Cooper realize she played the race card—and potentially put a man's life in danger—when she called the police in Central Park? Or did her conditioning enhance the danger she believed she was in when she called 911? Did she feel threatened because of his Blackness? Did she manipulate a situation to keep her dog unleashed? I wonder if Amy Cooper even knows.

Though racism still exists, it is much different today. In 1950, we weren't allowed in a public park. In 1950, we weren't allowed to live in white neighborhoods. In 1950 there was very little potential for interaction between the races. There was no opportunity for Amy Cooper to interact with Christian Cooper.

Today we can move to "white" suburbs; today we are able to get educations; today we are able to get good employment. We can live anywhere we can afford to live. We can put our children in any school district we can afford to live within. And that is how we are kept out: not being able to afford to live in areas with excellent public school districts. That's where the legacy of institutionalized racism still haunts us today.

Yet the microaggressions are constant reminders. We need to know about the Lolade Siyonbolas of the world, but do we subconsciously tell ourselves we do not belong at Yale? These are all reminders we are less than. The reminder that our claims do not matter. Unfortunately, in calling Black athletes like Colin Kaepernick un-American, President Trump did with words what firehoses did generations ago: it made us the bad guy in the culture war.

There is a cause-and-effect relationship. Words are the cause. The fight to keep confederate monuments honoring virulent segregationists and racists is the cause. Controlling our thinking is the effect. Not moving out of under-resourced neighborhoods is the effect.

Are we conditioned to be distracted by race? Granted, racism and its effects are very real. But it's one thing to be aware of (and annoyed by) this and quite another to be distracted by it. I realize now that the emphasis I placed on race in my teens and twenties distracted me from building the life I wanted to live. I did not have to waste time and energy looking at every perceived slight through a racial lens. When an elevator door closed on me, was it because the white guy didn't want to share the elevator with me? Or did they not notice I was rushing up to the elevator? Perceiving slights where none are intended doesn't get us anywhere and drains us of energy we can use to move forward in life.

I have a friend who complains his car insurance is higher than mine because he lives on Chicago's predominantly Black South Side. He says he can't buy a home on the north side of Chicago because he's Black. Bullshit, I tell him. He made a choice to live where he lived. He could've chosen to move anywhere he wanted. But he has been conditioned to live there because that is what his parents and grandparents did. Of course, my friend's conditioning is based on historical truths: Not terribly long ago, Black people were unable to buy homes in white communities and were victimized by redlining. But today, we can do anything we want to do *despite* institutionalized racism.

It is often easier to complain about things than to go out and get what you want. It can be easier to complain about your boss rather than going out and finding that new job. It can be easier to complain about how racism affects our ability to live the American Dream than it is to reach out and achieve it. It's not easy earning privilege for yourself and your children and grandchildren. But it is possible for Black Americans to build privilege. Even though we don't have the same head start that our white brothers and sisters do, that dream is out there for the taking. We can *live* it. My life proves that, yes, maybe we are a step or two or five behind, but with education, mindful decisions, and hard work, we can start bridging that gap today.

Our Black leaders rightfully demand more resources for underserved communities. Although that is a laudable goal, we shouldn't have to wait for white people to send us resources. Is it fair for our children in under-resourced schools to fall further behind as they wait for help that never comes? Do we have enough evidence that those resources are not coming? Are our children not better served by moving to areas where the resources are? We can choose to be victims of the system, or we can strive to succeed regardless. White communities are not holding us back; they are taking care of themselves and their families, and we should be doing the same.

We need to either create resources in our communities or do what my parents did and move to where the resources are. Maya Angelou is often attributed as saying, "Do the best you can until you know better. Then when you know better, do better." Let's acknowledge and fight racism. But let's also acknowledge that we are waiting for fairness in an unfair world. Waiting puts it on America to act appropriately. What if America never does? What will waiting for the rules to change do for you and your children and grandchildren? Is there any evidence that the powers that be are going to change the rules? While we fight the legacy of institutionalized racism, we can also work around it. My parents did it. I'm doing it. Millions of us are doing it. And you can do it too.

CHAPTER SIX

What Is Holding You Back from Your Dreams?

YOU SIT WHERE you are today because of the decisions you have made.

Let that sink in: *Every decision you have made has led you to where you are today.*

When I first heard self-improvement guru Lisa Nichols say this on the *School of Greatness* podcast with Lewis Howes,[19] it stopped me in my tracks. Lisa was talking about needing baby formula and diapers when she had only twelve dollars in her bank account and her fiancé was in jail. She looked in the mirror and realized it was her decision-making—not the fact that she was Black—that had put her where she was. Her Blackness didn't cause her to have twelve dollars in her bank account at that moment. Her sex didn't cause her to be humbled by her finances at that moment. She looked back at her decision-making: the relationship she chose, her under-employment and reliance on that relationship, put her in that position. The decision to have a baby with a man who didn't deserve her put her in that position. Lisa was standing in the consequences of her decisions. This can be a humbling realization if you are in difficult circumstances. But it's also a powerful one that provides you control over your life.

When I first heard Lisa's words, I had well over $30,000 in credit card debt and roughly $75,000 in IRS debt from my business. Her insights shifted my consciousness. *I put myself here—* my Blackness had nothing to do with my decision to charge a vacation to my credit card or to buy a BMW before paying down my IRS debt. Lisa Nichols's words gave me the power to know that if I want different results, I need to make different decisions.

Take a few moments and really look at where you are— what you have created. Your children. Your friends. Your home. There is plenty of good where you sit right now. Acknowledge that good. Acknowledge the work you've put into creating the life you have. Your decisions created that good. But also take a moment and look at where you "lack." What decisions did you make that produced those circumstances? Where could you make different decisions to create the life you want?

Reaping the Fruit of Sound Decisions

Once, when I was in my twelve-year-old son's room, I had what I can only describe as an out-of-body experience. It was cold and snowy outside, but in his room it was warm and cozy: baseball hats strewn all over, sports pennants on the walls, the bed chaotic with pillows and blankets and clothes. As we were hanging out, I was transported back to my own twelve-year-old self—secure in my room, safe at home with all my belongings around me, confident that there was food in the refrigerator downstairs. Then, as I got up to leave the room, I was transported back to the present.

I shook myself as I would after a dream and realized that I had created the security in my son's room by providing all this stuff: his access to electronics and the internet, his work with tutors via Zoom, his cozy cocoon of security in a safe, warm home. I was flooded with overwhelming gratitude for having been able to create this awesome space for him.

Of course, all of this was possible only because of the decisions my wife and I had made over the last ten years of our lives. We made sacrifices to get where we were. Seven years before that moment in my son's room, I had left a very comfortable job at a law firm to start my own firm and build my own culture. I was forty years old, and I thought if I didn't do it then, I may never do it. At the same time, we sold our Chicago home and moved to Northbrook, a suburb north of Chicago.

We very intentionally made the decision to move to an area with great school districts because we believe that education is key to opportunity. However, that move caused our mortgage to almost double at a time when my income was cut in half. I woke up most nights at three in the morning, staring at the red numbers of my alarm clock while remembering the red bank account numbers in my dreams. I managed our money, so it was on me to pay the mortgage and bills, including daycare for two kids. I can clearly remember the time I sat frozen in my home office, unable to write a mortgage check that was forty-nine days overdue. My wife, Amy, jumped into action and ordered me to sell stock here and transfer money there to get the mortgage paid. We'd pay ourselves back later.

We lived this way for years. Though we were in an affluent community, we often crossed our fingers that our debit card would cover the groceries. Our credit cards were at or near the max, so if we needed to pay for an emergency repair, I would have to pay cash.

As we endured this daily struggle, my wife asked a neighbor who owned his own law firm how long it took to get his footing when running his business. Her question seemed innocent enough to him, but I knew the desperation behind it. The constant worrying about money was hard to endure. This went on for three or four years. However, through all that stress, sleepless nights, and checking the Chase app on my phone at Target or a restaurant (I couldn't tell you why I chose *after* being in the restaurant to check my Chase app to see how much money we had—but this was a common occurrence) there was one constant: we knew we had made the right decision.

Success is *not* easy. We risked a lot to provide our children with what they have. Because we intentionally went out of our comfort zone early on, we are now in a position of comfort. Of course, my wife and I were able to do this because our parents gave us a head start. As I said earlier, my privilege—my children's privilege—is a consequence of decisions my parents made over forty years ago. Lisa Nichols is right that I sit where I am today because of the decisions I made. But it's equally true that my children sit where *they* are today because of decisions my parents made four decades ago.

Let's think back to the privilege race challenge I mentioned earlier in the book. The college-aged kids who were fortunate enough to take steps forward in the privilege race had those opportunities because of the decisions their parents made. I work hard for the privilege my children have, as my parents did before me. That work started long before I had children, because I wanted to duplicate the privilege I saw my parents earn for my sister and me. As a parent, I now see the ingredients involved with providing for children: a mix of mindset, hard work, and self-investment, combined with some sleepless nights, sprinkled with a few calculated risks. It's far easier to write off another person's privilege and our own lack of it due to something outside of ourselves. But if we choose to have children we cannot afford to feed, is society failing us or are we failing our children? To climb the privilege ladder, we have to recognize that some of these circumstances have little to do with race. However, we can't completely discount race, because in my grandparents' generation, race did limit our options.

There comes a time when we need to decide what we want for ourselves and our children. For example, if you live in an area with poorly performing schools, every day that your child stays at that underperforming, under-resourced school, they fall further behind. Your child needs an education *today.* Do you choose to stay where you are and hope the government steps up to the plate with resources, or will you shop for a better school district? If you shop for the nicest car or clothes you can afford, why would you not shop for the best school district you can afford?

How My Parents' Decisions Shaped My World

I grew up in Elmhurst, Illinois, about sixteen miles west of Chicago. My parents were from the suburbs just east of Elmhurst, which were dominated by blue-collar jobs (back when those jobs were plentiful). Most of my grandparents, aunts, and uncles worked in factories; my grandfather and aunt both worked as cab drivers. They all worked hard, and they all put food on the table, but they lived paycheck to paycheck with no savings.

From where my parents were raised, one travels fifteen minutes west on St. Charles Road, over two large highways separating Cook County from DuPage, and you enter the leafy green canopy of trees that make up Elmhurst. My parents purchased a tiny three-bedroom, one-bathroom home on the edge of town. It was the crappiest home on the block, but it was in Elmhurst, which meant it was in a great school district.

When he was not working at Illinois Bell, my father set to work fixing our house with his two hands. He painted the exterior and put up aluminum siding (a big deal in 1980). The house initially came with a dilapidated one-car garage out back; when they were able to afford it, my parents had it replaced with a new two-car garage. To save money, my dad got a dumpster, grabbed a sledgehammer, and took the old garage down *himself* on a Saturday. After a couple of years of constant work and investment, the crappiest house on the block became the nicest one. By the time I was in my teens, my family was not using wooden spools as furniture anymore and was firmly within America's middle class. My sister and I did not want for anything. We had a nice home in a great suburb with excellent schools; we were able to go on vacations; we had computers, video games, televisions in our rooms. We were given money to go to the movies or hang out with friends.

When you grow up with this kind of privilege, you don't realize how good you have it. We knew our schools were good because teachers and school administrators constantly told us about the opportunities this education would provide. But we didn't know that jumping on a bike and riding over to Alex's house to play video games was a "privilege." As far as we were concerned, that was just life.

After graduating high school, I went to college, and I don't recall having choice in that matter—just like many of my friends. Going to college wasn't just expected, it was required (as it is for my children). Had I grown up in a community where this wasn't the norm, I may not have gone to college at all—even with the same intellectual ability.

My parents sacrificed mightily so that I could get a good education. They insisted that I grow up in a community where going to college was expected, and doing so meant moving to Elmhurst. This may not seem like a sacrifice, but a mixed-race couple certainly raised eyebrows in the Reagan-era Republican suburbs. We learned early on to keep our chins up in the face of stares and whispers.

At the same time, my father was dealing with coworkers who didn't want him to work alongside them, let alone advance, because of the color of his skin. Every night when my father returned home from work, I heard him talk about "that motherfucker Steerhoff," so much so that I thought *motherfucker* was Steerhoff's first name. My father had to tolerate racist taunts day in and day out at the office. If he were to complain, he risked losing his job and, by extension, my own opportunities for a bright future.

And it wasn't just my father who had to deal with this. I remember the word *nigger* being hurled at me from passing cars as I walked to school. When I would report this to my father, his reaction wasn't anger so much as weariness—it was as though he expected that kind of treatment.

One day, my father was moving his bike from the garage to our backyard shed when a police officer jumped out of his squad car, ran up to the front door, and informed my mother that a Black man had just stolen a bike from her garage. Looking back on it now, I'm glad he rang the doorbell and got yelled at by my mother rather than confront my father—because we know all too well how such confrontations can end.

Unfortunately, this kind of behavior wasn't limited to the Elmhurst of the 1980s. In 2000, one of the first phone calls I received as a lawyer was from a very dark-skinned friend who was also raised in Elmhurst. A police officer had stopped him for speeding and called for five other squad cars for backup for this minor infraction. My friend was taken from his car and thrown onto the hood. Ultimately no ticket was given. Would this have happened to one of our white friends? Privilege isn't only moving to and living in towns like Elmhurst; privilege is not having five police officers embarrass and harass you because of your skin color.

The Value of a Forward-Thinking Mindset

My parents stretched to afford that small and run-down house in Elmhurst. They both worked long hours, racking up all the overtime they could, and put most of what they earned back into that small home, fixing up the exterior and yard so "the Black family" didn't cause property values to go down (even though several white families also had rundown homes on the block).

I sit in gratitude remembering that mindset. I recognize the opportunity my parents' decisions afforded me. I didn't have to worry about earning money at eighteen years old. I never worried about paying bills growing up. I always had food in the house. I lived in an excellent school district—where the public schools were better than the private ones. I had access to a tutor and was able to take prep courses for the ACT (which made a distinct difference on the test). By having two parents in the home—and dual incomes—the economics of running a household was easier. I had two parents modeling hard work and saw that hard work meant monetary rewards.

Notice that those opportunities have nothing to do with the color of my skin. None of those opportunities had to do with race. They were the consequences of the decisions my parents made. It's not easy having to tolerate casual overt racism while in your front yard in the house that you sacrificed to pay for. Yet it's those decisions that made the privilege my children enjoy possible. That pebble thrown into a pond creates ripples. My sitting in my son's warm room, drunk in gratitude, while it was below zero outside, with two feet of snow on the ground during a global pandemic with food in the fridge and money in the bank, is the ripple of the pebble my parents threw into the pond forty years ago.

I should note that my wife's white parents had more opportunities than my own parents. My parents belonged to the first generation of Black Americans widely able to build wealth and leave a legacy for their children outside the shadow of Jim Crow. By contrast, my wife's family had been able to build up and pass down wealth over several generations. Two quick points on this: First, as my parents show, it is possible to change the trajectory of a family's wealth in a single generation. Second, plenty of white kids were less privileged than I was growing up in Elmhurst. Race plays a role in getting into the room, but it's not the only key to the door.

Wealth is not the only thing passed down from generation to generation; mentality is as well. To break the generational curse of slavery and segregation, we must be conscious of how we've been conditioned to think about ourselves.

RACE PLAYS A ROLE IN GETTING INTO THE ROOM, BUT IT'S NOT THE ONLY KEY TO THE DOOR

Imagine showing up at the Tour de France without a bicycle, having only ever seen people ride bikes from a distance, while everyone else has been competing in the event for *centuries*. Then, *after being forced to give you a bike*, your competitors shake their heads because you have been allowed to compete. Your competitor will win the race that year, but next year, you'll show up with a better bike. You'll still get blown away and laughed at, but the following year you'll be in better shape, having ridden a better bicycle over the last year. In year three you're even more competitive. By year ten, you're finishing in the top ten, and by year fifteen you're on the cusp of winning first place.

But to get there, *you first have to decide you want to be in the race.*

CHAPTER SEVEN

Race Is Not Holding You Back

WE DESERVE to be in the race. In 2024, race does not keep us from privilege. It is not 1950. We can get an education. We can go to college. College, although certainly not affordable, is available through scholarships and grants. That college experience can help children see how large the world is rather than knowing only the confinement of your neighborhood or town where you grew up.

The government no longer segregates us and no longer limits where we can live and raise a family. Employers can no longer keep us out of employment because of our skin color. We can go into any restaurant, hotel, tavern, waiting room, or restroom we desire.

We keep ourselves out of these places. Our conditioning keeps us segregated.

This happens in white communities too. Plenty of white people stay in the communities in which they grew up. Many people do what their parents did. That is what people do. It is not a race thing. It's a comfort thing. Humans seek comfort. And we use the past to set our comfort level.

That is what many people fight for: the comfort of what they knew growing up. We want the comfort of what we know: the good ole days with grandma cooling an apple pie on the windowsill, when children play outside safely and come in when the street lights come on.

But the world changes, and those days are behind us. Kids aren't playing kick the can in front yards anymore, opting for being on electronics in dark basements. Kids don't come in when the streetlights come on. Kids have easier access to guns and drugs. Kids play video games and watch media that shows them how to use both—at a young age. This is no longer the age of *House Party* or *Sixteen Candles*, where parents go out of town and high schoolers invade the home with beer and music. We're now in an age where kids get online with the savvy to meet people in different towns, area codes, and states.

Just like the days of kick the can are over, so are the days of segregated restrooms, waiting rooms, buses, hotels, and restaurants. Sundown towns—cities where Black people are not allowed after dark—no longer exist.

Although we don't want to go back to the good ole days of segregation, as humans, we seek the comfort of what we know. Neighborhoods we grew up in, schools we attended, meals we ate growing up as children, and people we knew.

But does racism play a role in having children before having an education (or earning a stable living with a career)? What opportunity does an eighteen-year-old have to build a foundation to afford a child? I had my first child at thirty-five years old. I had seventeen years after high school to build a foundation of education and then a résumé and job experience before I had my son. In those seventeen years, I built not only some monetary wealth—buying a home, having savings—but also a solid foundation having been a lawyer for nearly ten years. That is the world my children were born into. However, if I had had children when I was an eighteen-year-old, I would have had to drop out of college, would have had no savings, and would have had no home other than my parents' home. I would have had little education and less opportunity to achieve one because I was caring for a child before I had opportunity to invest in myself.

It's important to take care of yourself before you have to take care of a helpless child.

Yes, racism exists. But when we decide to have children without personal economic stability, without a good job or career, without a stable partner, and without an education, is it the effects of racism holding us back? Or is it our decision-making?

Changing Our Response to Racism

By changing our response to racism, we can ensure that we are less affected by it. Take, for example, the steps we teach our children to take if they're pulled over by a police officer. To get the best outcome in those situations, we tell our children to do the following:

- If it's nighttime, put the dome light on so the police officer can see into the vehicle.

- Keep your hands on the steering wheel at all times so the police officer can see them.

- Be polite and respond to the police officer with "yes sir/ ma'am" or "no sir/ma'am."

- When reaching to get your license, registration, or anything else inside the vehicle, announce to the police officer what you intend on doing with your hands.

- Record the encounter.

- Always remember that the goal is for you and the police officer to both leave the situation peacefully, so act accordingly.

Racism might get us pulled over, but how we respond to that racism will go a long way toward affecting the outcome.

We teach our children to put themselves in the best position so they won't be the next Tamir Rice or Philando Castile (not that either of them did anything wrong when they were confronted by police).

Knowing that your response affects the outcome of a situation changes the dynamic by giving you some control. Responding to a police officer by mouthing off will surely take the control of your immediate future out of your hands and place it into the hands of the police. A more intentional response with a desired outcome in mind (e.g., driving away from the situation unharmed) ensures that you retain some control over your fate.

The same principle applies to where you sit today. Recognizing that your present circumstances are due to the decisions you've made helps you take control by moving you from the passenger back to the driver's seat of your life.

Mindset Equals Control; Control Equals Power

"Until you make the unconscious conscious, it will direct your life and you will call it fate." Attributed to Carl Jung,[20] this quote reflects a certain truth, which is part of the message of this book. Take back your power by considering that unconscious thoughts and beliefs are what put you where you are today. Take back control by recognizing that your conditioning has you sitting where you are today. Take back control by knowing that by doing things differently you'll get different outcomes.

The police officer who pulled you over is the stimulus, and when your response consists of mouthing off, yelling at the police officer's racism and getting belligerent could result in a $200.00 ticket for having a taillight out Alternatively, you could have a pleasant exchange with the officer, where they let you know the taillight is out and you let them know you had no clue your taillight was out (How could you?—how often do you check your own taillight?). You share a laugh, and the officer, after getting your promise to fix it, allows you to go on your merry way. That's your response affecting the outcome.

Mindset going into a situation affects the outcome. Having the mindset that all police officers are racist can result in a negative outcome because that belief will most likely affect your response. You'll go into the situation expecting a negative outcome—and then you'll get exactly what you expect.

Acknowledgment of our unconscious provides awareness. Our awareness controls our mindset. Our mindset controls our response.

Our response gives us control over the situation. We lose control of the situation when we lose control of our response. In other words: we lose control when we lose control. I encourage you to be more mindful of your reactions to stimuli. Whether that be your child throwing his socks all over the house, a police officer pulling you over for no apparent reason, someone cutting you off on the highway, or the alarm going off at 5:45 a.m. for a workout, consider your response. Who do you want to be? If you want to look like Michael B. Jordan shirtless, then you get up and get to the gym. If you want to look like Rerun from *What's Happening!* then you turn over and go back to sleep. Our response to stimulus affects who we are. We visualize who we want to be and act accordingly when stimulus hits.

> ## ACKNOWLEDGMENT OF OUR UNCONSCIOUS PROVIDES AWARENESS. OUR AWARENESS CONTROLS OUR MINDSET. OUR MINDSET CONTROLS OUR RESPONSE.

Lisa Nichols reminds us that it was her decisions that put her in the position she was in when she was overweight, had a fiancé in jail, and had only twelve dollars in her account and had to buy food and diapers for her newborn. She could blame the outside and the fact that she is a Black woman in America and *that's* what caused her to be in her difficult situation. Or she could take control of her life and make different decisions so she had more money in her account. She could find a partner who was available and not in danger of going to jail. She could intentionally eat differently and move her body differently to lose excess weight. She could make small promises to herself, and by keeping them, gain self-confidence.

Amelia Earhart is attributed with saying, "The most effective way to do it, is to do it." So I write. So I get down on the ground and pound out twenty push-ups. So I eat my apple. So I get up early and make the time to do the things that I tell myself are important. I make the time to be the person I am becoming.

That guy, the guy I will be in five years, is the guy I visualize when I encounter a situation and have a choice in who I am being.[21]

I'll still watch *Law & Order*. I'll still eat that awesome cheese and caramel popcorn. I'll still have one or two (okay, four) more cocktails than my doctor would like. I like doing these things, so I'll do them—but I am mindful of these choices. And I'll be compassionate with myself and remind myself that it's okay to not do things at times, as long as I am doing the things to get to that best version of myself. I know this to be true not because I am perfect. I know this because of my flaws.

Does racism truly hold us back, or can our response

to it effect better outcomes? A poor response will lead to a poor outcome. A good, wise response will lead to either a good outcome or one where we leave the experience behind and chalk it up as another unfortunate by-product of living in America. The issue is not whether we should have to live dealing with racist crap we should not have to deal with.

The issue is how we will thrive regardless.

Negotiating Socioeconomic Blackness

Once you decide to thrive rather than just survive, your circumstances will begin to change. For example, if your goal is to climb the socioeconomic ladder, you'll see that happen rung by rung. With hard work, the bank account balance that usually dips into the negative will stay positive. You will set up savings and investment accounts, and you will watch them grow. Now you can direct the energy that you used to spend stressing out about your checking balance toward working on goals. As you work on your goals, opportunities will arise.

And as you climb that ladder, ask yourself this question: Is class more important than race?

Is Michael Jordan Black? I ask because it seemed like white people in the 1980s and 1990s didn't think of him as Black but as rich and popular. Growing up, friends told me they didn't consider me Black. I even heard from some Black people that I wasn't "Black enough." Why? Because my family started building wealth? Because I was "articulate"? Because I was smart? The assumption that making money, speaking well, and being intelligent are somehow not "Black" is the result of racist conditioning.

Do we really think that to understand Blackness we need to be poor? That middle-class Black people are somehow less Black and rich Black people aren't Black at all? Does our Blackness slowly disappear the higher we ascend the economic ladder? Does "keeping it real" actually mean "staying poor"? Is getting an education "bougie"? Is making a good living the same as selling out? Unfortunately, we've been conditioned to believe that the answer to each of these questions is yes. For example, this conditioning can be seen in the title of the TV show *Black-ish*. It's a great show, but the whole premise is that moving up the economic ladder makes you "Blackish" rather than Black.

For centuries, we have been taught that Blackness equals dangerousness. We die at the hands of police because they are afraid of our Blackness. Why else does the National Guard get called out to a Black Lives Matter rally but not to a predominantly white insurrection at the Capitol? If we lose our Blackness as we become increasingly professional, is that because we are seen as less and less dangerous?

Too often, we keep ourselves from inhabiting more

comfortable spaces because we believe they aren't "our place" as Black people. For example, when we were dating, my wife's family is affluent and they once put us up at a Four Seasons in California. I was so damned intimidated that I half-expected people to hand me their keys thinking I was the valet. I walked around the buffet warily, waiting for someone to say, "Fetch me some butter, boy!"

Of course, none of the things I feared would happen happened. Nobody thought I was the valet, and I ate at the buffet without incident. But I had walked into that resort with so much baggage in addition to my literal luggage that it affected the quality my trip. The entire time I was at the Four Seasons, I had the nagging feeling that I did not belong.

That mindset has to stop.

The irony about my own mindset was that I was twenty-nine years old. I already lived a life where I saw my parents work hard and ascend the economic ladder due to that hard work. I gave myself permission to build enough success to be solidly middle class or maybe even upper-middle class.

I did *not* give myself permission to be wealthy. I did not give myself permission to be truly affluent. My Blackness did not give me that permission. My Blackness did not allow for doors to open above the doors I had already seen open. My parents were careful to open doors for me and my sister and we were allowed in—if not initially welcomed. The next doors I was solidly against going into. I told myself because of my Blackness and its socioeconomic component, I did not belong.

I was totally uncomfortable and "forced" (who can be "forced" to stay at a Four Seasons?) outside my comfort zone and learned that I brought a lot of baggage into that resort with me that wasn't true.

There may have been people or families within the resort who believed I didn't belong because of my skin color. Just like there were people and families who didn't believe I belonged in Elmhurst because of my skin color.

Ultimately, those people didn't keep my parents out of Elmhurst, so why should they keep me out of Beverly Hills?

If *we* believe that, then we won't move to the Elmhursts of the world. If *we* believe that, then we won't move to Beverly Hills or the Hamptons or some other uber-affluent zip code and we'll subconsciously sabotage ourselves. If *we* believe that, we'll stay in our present circumstances and lament that we can't move beyond what we already have. And that's bullshit.

When we walk into rooms, race plays a role. Some people will look at us and question whether we belong in the room. Just like Elmhurst or the Four Seasons, the issue is not about what they think but about what we think when we enter these rooms. Do we believe we belong in the room and therefore stay?

Start off your adult life in a position of strength—by getting an education. That education provides opportunity. You will earn a career rather than a job. You will learn how to invest in yourself and in assets and gain upward mobility and financial freedom. Getting an education will fuel confidence when you first arrive in the room. Get that education. Give your children that education.

Our collective goal can be giving ourselves and our children—and their children—the head start in the privilege race that affluent white children have. It's not our Blackness that keeps our children away from those steps forward in the privilege race; it's our conditioning about what that Blackness means. Our conditioning affects our decisions. Our decisions affect our children's opportunities. We can make mindful decisions creating positive consequences. We can make mindful decisions creating the future we want. Race only affects our decision-making when *we* allow it to. The conversation we have with ourselves is the most important conversation we have. Start having the conversation that we belong in rooms with doctors, lawyers, wealth managers, entrepreneurs, bankers, and CEOs, and we'll find ourselves and our children in those rooms.

My life is evidence that Black and brown people can overcome socioeconomic circumstances to create more wealth, abundance, opportunity, and freedom. And I am not an anomaly. Millions of Black people have forged paths up the socioeconomic ladder. You, too, can be one of those millions.

CHAPTER EIGHT

Creating Different Consequences

LIVING IN CHICAGO, one of my favorite times is when we get a snowstorm—the first one at least. I open the curtains and watch the snow come down outside. I build a fire, grab a blanket, and lie on the couch as I read a book and watch the storm outside. This is one of my favorite times because this is when I feel most grateful. I feel grateful for my home warmed by heat, the refrigerator full of food, and knowing my family is safe within the walls of our home. As I watch the blizzard rage outside, I am so very grateful for these basics that everything else becomes gravy.

But again, I would not be in the position I am in today if it were not for decisions my parents made long ago. I am not special. Had I grown up in an area where gangs are the norm, I would have been in a gang. I just did what the people around me did. There was no special spark within me saying, "Get an education, become a lawyer, and live a certain lifestyle!" Had my parents lived in a different community, I may have been in the same courtroom, but as a defendant, waiting for my case to be called. I recognize that.

The area my parents intentionally chose to live in was a community of people who valued education and the opportunity education provides. As I got older, the programming from my childhood—to value education and the opportunity it provides—put me next to other people who valued education and its opportunity. I found myself sitting next to people finishing college and preparing to take the LSAT, sitting next to people figuring out their first year of law school, sitting next to people preparing to take the bar exam, sitting next to people waiting for their case to be called in court so they could appear on behalf of their client.

Yet I was the one who sat through four years of college classes. *I* took the LSAT. *I* took three years of law school classes and studied for three years to get into a position to take the bar exam. *I* found a job. *I* learned how to practice law.

Look at where you sit right now. Yes, to some extent, your upbringing put you there because that provided you with a value system. It put you where you are because you were conditioned to see the world in a certain way. Your conditioning tells you that you deserve to be in your seat because your parents, your aunts, your grandparents, your friends, your village are all similarly situated. If they deserve to be where they are, why is it you deserve more?

But my parents decided they deserved something different, and they intentionally broke from what was expected. In making decisions intended to help their children, they changed the trajectory for generations.

Our decision-making has us where we are. There is a consequence for every decision we make.

Own your decisions.

Own those consequences.

Once you own your consequences, you can create new consequences.

The Effects of Racism on Consequences

Recently, I had a conversation with a twenty-year-old Black woman involved in a car accident. Another person totaled her car and fled the scene. She did not have a way to get to work and was in danger of losing her job. She was upset because she had chosen not to pay her $98 car insurance premium the month before because she wanted to give her three children Christmas gifts instead. I get it: Christmas presents are much more fun than car insurance premiums—until someone crashes into your car and flees the scene, leaving your car destroyed. Now her insurance would not cover her damages because her policy lapsed. As a single mother of three, she was desperate for help because she had to earn money to put food on the table for her kids.

I had only bad news. Yes, I could get money for her, but it would require filing a lawsuit to recoup her damages. We could get the money to fix her car, but it would take at least twelve months to get the money in her pocket. The problem is that she needed money today; she needed money to fix her car so she could go to work to make ends meet. Without that car, her life could unravel quickly. She was upset. She was the victim of someone else's decision to drive recklessly and now she and her small family had to pay the consequences for someone else's action.

She was paying for the consequences of someone else's poor decision-making. But she also had to accept responsibility for her own decisions that put her in the tough spot she was in.

Her lapsed insurance resulted in no money to get her car fixed, which meant she couldn't get to work. Not having a way to get to work caused a double whammy: she had no income coming in and because she wasn't reporting to work, she lost her job.

No income meant no money to feed her children, no money to heat the apartment in a harsh Chicago winter, no money to pay for electricity. The fallout from not having an extra $98 to pay a car insurance premium was catastrophic. Her life was already difficult as a single mother earning fifteen dollars an hour that had to go toward a home, food, electricity, and heat for three kids. Her existence was difficult before her car was wrecked and this one setback—which should have been a small one—made her life impossible.

When I was twenty years old, I didn't have money saved either. I was in college and my parents funded my life. The plan was for me to get a college degree and then they would slowly shut off the faucet that watered my lifestyle I would fend for myself after I had my college diploma. But even after I received my college degree, my parents were my safety net.

That safety net included a car they purchased and insured. The safety net included medical insurance they provided. The safety net included emergency funding for unexpected events. They made the decision that I would be given the opportunity to work toward my law degree before I had to figure things out on my own. Their decision was borne from their belief that I would be able to better fend for myself—earn sufficient money—with an education.

Unfortunately, that twenty-year-old woman did not have the safety net that I had, meaning she was on her own to try to figure it out. That is not her fault. I would not have been able to figure it out at that age without help from my parents.

I understand my good fortune to have had the parents I had.

I want to write "I understand my privilege." But is it truly privilege? Is the fact that my parents made certain decisions to put me through college so I had the opportunity to earn a better living a "privilege" or is it the consequences of their decisions? Isn't privilege something unearned? Good health can be a privilege—being born with a heart, lungs, liver, and kidneys that all work; two arms and two legs. But even health in many respects is earned: if you eat junk food every day and don't exercise, after years of that approach, the consequence can be failing health.

Yet I did have privilege because I didn't earn the ability to go to college without having to pay for it. But my parents' hard work earned me that privilege. They made decisions, and the consequences of their decisions led to my privilege.

That's what we forget. Too often, we look at others who have more than us and sneer at their privilege, yet we don't acknowledge the decisions their parents or grandparents made so they could have that privilege.

We, too, can own that privilege. Our children can certainly own that privilege. Once we own that this privilege is not a result of our race but rather a result of our decisions, we can move toward it rather than sneering at those who have it.

I am a Black man who had the privilege of going to college and law school not because of affirmative action but because of the decisions my parents made. The woman in the hit-and-run wasn't uninsured because of racism but because of her decision not to pay her premium.

She put herself in the position of having to make that decision. *She* decided to have multiple children while she was still a child. Her decisions were based on her conditioning: She saw people who had children young rather than investing in education. I would not have been able to take care of a child at twenty years old. It was difficult enough taking care of my son when I was a thirty-five-year-old lawyer. An education, a solid job, a good partner, a suitable place to live—checking these things off the list before having children makes it much more likely that the children you *do* have won't live in poverty.

ONCE WE OWN THAT THIS PRIVILEGE IS NOT A RESULT OF OUR RACE BUT RATHER A RESULT OF OUR DECISIONS, WE CAN MOVE TOWARD IT, RATHER THAN SNEERING AT THOSE WHO HAVE IT.

When my wife and I had our first child, I was already a lawyer, and my wife, who has a master's degree, was working as a social worker. We owned our home and had some savings.

Even then, our expenses increased so much after Sammy was born that we had to tap our savings every month to make ends meet. If two educated thirty-five-year-old professionals had difficulty affording one child, just imagine what it was like for the single twenty-year-old woman earning fifteen dollars an hour.

It is not prophesied anywhere that people with Black and brown skin must live in poverty. But when people with Black and brown skin who live in poverty have children, those children will almost certainly live in poverty. This raises the question: Are Black and brown children living in poverty because they are Black and brown or because they are born into poverty?

Our skin color is *one* of the reasons so many of us are born into poverty. But we don't have to stay there. Black and brown people are no longer condemned to live the lives that our grandparents were forced to live. We must look in the mirror and own our decisions to forge a better life.

It's easy for the twenty-year-old woman whose uninsured car was destroyed to blame her predicament on someone else's, or society's, bad acts. But the real responsibility lies with her and her decisions. Other twenty-year-old Black women have had their cars damaged in an accident, called their insurance company, gotten their car repaired, and forgotten entirely about the situation in less than a month. So

Blackness, certainly, is not the issue here.

That is how racism can pervade our consciousness. Did you lose your job because of your skin color or were there a host of other decisions that led to that consequence? I'm not negating racism. Just like the car crash in the previous example, the woman would not have been in the predicament she was in but for the crash. But her precrash decision not to pay her car insurance made her bad situation even worse, not her Blackness.

I have made plenty of bad decisions myself. I bought more home than I could afford when my income was cut in half, and I chose to pay my mortgage rather than my taxes. Had I continued down that path, my business could have shut down and I could have gone to jail; my wife may have had to sell the house and move elsewhere without my help. Those would have been the consequences of my decision but not of my Blackness. One might argue that my Blackness makes it more likely that I would end up in prison than a similarly situated white guy, but it would still be my own decision-making that put me in that position.

What decision-making do we engage in that keeps us down? Does having children young and outside of marriage help or hurt our ability to transcend racism? Does not graduating high school or getting an education help or hurt our ability to transcend racism? These are two simple things that *we* control. The decision to get a high school diploma and not have children before we get that diploma is 100 percent within our own control. Blackness has no effect on those two decisions.

Racism can affect where we go to high school or college and the people around us. The effect of institutionalized racism plays a role in our opportunities in terms of the bias of a hiring manager or other students within higher education classrooms. But those opportunities will be even more limited if we choose to have children before we can afford them. Those opportunities will become even more limited if we choose not to graduate high school and move on to college or technical school.

When you find yourself on that high school graduation stage, you have another decision to make. Racism does not play a role in your decision. Do you move on to college or technical school? If you choose yes, you are more likely to create a stable life for yourself where you are able to withstand the consequences of a random racist act against you. Just like having car insurance helps create the ability to withstand the consequences of a random collision totaling your car.

I don't want to minimize racism and its effects on society and suggest that having car insurance will magically cure racism. However, should we choose to thrive, rather than just survive, we need to focus on the impact our decision-making has on the consequences we ultimately produce. That gives *us* control rather than others.

So what will you choose to do: thrive today or lament what could have been if only racism didn't exist? If you choose the latter, remember that the consequences of your choice will likely be felt by your children and your children's children. What you decide to do today can reverberate across *generations*. The cavalry is not coming to save us from racism, but when we accept the fact that our own decisions have profound consequences, we become our *children's* cavalry. We make decisions today that will put them in a better school district tomorrow.

If complaining about structural racism in the past has not changed underperforming school districts, will complaining about racism in that particular school district get my child the resources they need *today*, or will moving to a better school district get my child those resources?

Yes, racism exists in American society. But there is a way forward. Working toward abolishing racism is a goal that we should continue pursuing. But we should also recognize that outside of racism, our decisions control our consequences. Let's empower each other to make decisions that lead to the consequences we seek so that those consequences get us closer to our goal—our North Star. When we are intentional about making decisions to get us to those goals, we'll be better equipped to shrug off the racist acts when they happen.

CHAPTER NINE

What Do You Want Out of Life?

"Would you tell me, please, which way
I ought to go from here?"'
"That depends a good deal on where
you want to get to," said the Cat.
"I don't much care where," said Alice.
"Then it doesn't matter which way you go," said the Cat.
"So long as I get somewhere,"
added Alice as an explanation.
"Oh, you're sure to do that," said the Cat,
"if you only walk long enough."

—CONVERSATION BETWEEN ALICE AND
THE CHESHIRE CAT IN ALICE IN WONDERLAND

I WOKE UP once again at 5:00 a.m. I trudged to the bathroom in the dark, took a quick shower, and got ready for another day of work. I put on my suit and left for work by 5:45 as my family continued sleeping. It was dark outside as I began my commute into Chicago. My neighborhood was quiet but for the paperman throwing newspapers on driveways. I'd had to call the *Chicago Tribune* begging for an earlier delivery so I could get my paper on the way to the office rather than reading yesterday's news when I returned home.

By 7:00 a.m., I was at my desk working. I went to court, I participated in depositions, I went to lunches with people who sent me business and took others to lunch I wanted to get business from. I worked until at least 6:30 in the evening, and after my commute, returned home at 7:30. My daughter was in bed. I'd take my suit off and get to spend a few quiet minutes with her as she drifted off to sleep. I'd get to see my son for about an hour. After that, I'd get to see my wife. She wanted to talk about my day or talk about hers, but by the time I got home I was so exhausted that I had nothing left to give her.

I loved the work. It was nice to see my business grow. But what was I really doing? In the long Chicago winter, I'd find myself driving to work in the dark and driving home in the dark. By February a certain exhaustion set in while the stress about money kept me up at night. And somewhere mixed with all the stress of running and building a business while practicing law, somewhere, deep, deep within me, was the question: Is this what you really wanted?

Was I having fun? No. Absolutely not. There were great things about it, it was fun at times, but it was drudgery. I wasn't seeing my kids. I wasn't connecting with my wife. I wasn't being a father who was present for his family. Sure, I was building a business and there was excitement to that—but was I living the life I wanted to live?

For a long time, I ignored that quiet inner whisper. I was far too overwhelmed by day-to-day stressors to pay it any mind.

Then in October 2016, as the Chicago Cubs were marching to the World Series, what was ultimately a good thing happened: I was knocked off my feet by a pulmonary embolism.

The week before it happened, I was on trial, trying a medical malpractice case in front of a jury. It was tough and exciting at the same time. It had taken six weeks of work to get myself ready for this two-week trial, but once that jury was picked and after the first few words of my opening statement, muscle memory kicked in and it was exhilarating. I was amped on adrenaline and felt great.

But in order to get to those moments, I had had six weeks of twelve-to-fourteen-hour days. It was not fun. I didn't see my family. I didn't see friends. Much of my practice was put on hold so I could work on this single case. The case was important and it deserved the attention, but so did my children and wife. So did I. That whisper asked: *Is this what you wanted?*

But I couldn't hear that question. I was in front of this jury presenting my case. I felt good about most of the evidence as it was presented to the jury. It culminated the Friday before Columbus Day; the last witness the defense put on that day was one of their expert witnesses. I was prepared for him and politely gutted him with my questions. Prior to this cross-examination, I took his deposition and saw in his body language he wasn't terribly comfortable in his opinions. In front of the jury, I asked questions he looked uncomfortable answering, and it worked. The jury could tell—he squirmed when he helped the defense and made admissions that helped our case. It was my Tom Cruise / Jack Nicholson "You can't handle the truth!" moment, without the yelling.

My clients hugged me when the jury left for the day. It was one of my best cross-examinations ever, in a big spot.

And twenty-four hours later, I found myself in a cold hospital room, with dangerous blood clots in both legs.

The symptoms had started earlier in the week. My calves were swollen and in tremendous pain. I take pride in my pain tolerance and fought through it, working my ass off and then taking Tylenol and elevating my legs when I got home. Something was wrong, but it would have to wait another week and we'd figure it out. My only thought was getting this verdict.

The Saturday after the cross-examination, I spent the day in the office working, and that evening, got home, showered, and ran across the street for a friend's child's birthday party. At the party, my calves were in flames and twice their normal size. After looking at my legs, my friends ordered me to go to urgent care. The urgent care doctor sent me straight to the ER so I could get ultrasounds done on my legs.

I waited in the ER for hours that Saturday night, watching the Cubs beat the San Francisco Giants in the playoffs, frustrated with the staff because *I had work to do!* When the doctor finally saw me, she told me I had dangerous blood clots in both legs. She told me I could no longer walk—for fear the clot would break off and end up in my lungs (which it eventually did).

I found myself lying in a hospital bed, tossing and turning, worrying about how the next week would look. That Sunday morning, I emailed and called defense counsel from my hospital bed. We were so close to the end after two weeks of trial—yet did my body have the ability to go on? Would my body allow me to get that verdict?

With the specific question, "Would my body allow me to get this verdict?" came the larger question, "Would my body allow me to do this work?" and I struggled with that question for months. After leaving the hospital, anxiety hit. The anxiety was crippling at times. Would I be able to earn a living for my wife and children? Would I be able to maintain an office from a hospital bed? Would I be alive to see my kids graduate high school and walk my daughter down the aisle at her wedding?

For years I told myself that although I may not be the smartest person in the room, nobody would outwork me. Now I questioned whether I could work like that anymore. Did I even *want* to work like that anymore? Did I have to give up lawyering altogether or could I give up the type of lawyering that had me at a desk for so long that severe blood clots formed in my legs? I loved my business, but did I love what the work meant for me? Did I have what it takes? Did I even want to have what it takes?

The questions exhausted me. I had incapacitating anxiety. I was only comfortable on my couch, with my legs elevated and Xanax in my bloodstream. When I went to the office, most days I was lightheaded and had shortness of breath—two symptoms that could mean the blood clots had gone to my lungs—and I had to figure out whether I was going back to the ER so the doctors could take a look and see if I was suffering another anxiety attack or if it was the pulmonary embolism.

Though I didn't realize it at the time, these frightening moments ended up being a great thing for me. Life slowed down enough for me to finally consider that nagging inner question: *Is this what you wanted?*

I looked around and I saw my kids again. I saw my wife again. I saw that walking my daughter down the aisle one day was more important to me than winning any trial. I started to really question what I wanted from life rather than just blindly continuing on the path that had put me in a hospital bed, afraid and wondering how I was going to feed my family. *A path that actually put my life in danger.*

Although it didn't happen overnight, I made decisions to change my life. I decided to work on different types of cases that had different demands on me, to hire more staff and attorneys to take many of those demands so I could spend more time with my family.

And *that* is what I wanted from life. I want to be able to work yet have the freedom to spend time with my family. I want to be able to be a lawyer *and* write. I want to be able to travel yet have the staff that takes care of our clients while I'm away from the office. I also want the ability to communicate and take care of their needs from San Diego as easily as when I'm in the office in Chicago. I want to go to Little League softball and baseball games. I want to sleep in once in a while and walk downstairs in shorts and a T-shirt and get to work. I want to be able to take a break from work and have lunch with my wife. I want to write a book!

Deciding What You Want Out of Life

What do *you* want out of life? Go back to chapter 2 where you wrote out what you wanted and review your list. Do other things come up? Of course you wrote the big things, but did you write the small? The big things, like a million dollars in your bank account; the small things, like a tidier house; and the medium-sized things, like going to Paris or the Super Bowl one day. Just make sure these things are what *you* want, not things your parents or friends want for you. And keep writing. Don't worry about how outrageous your wants might seem; do not attach judgment to anything you write. Just keep flowing. Get after it. And don't forget to have fun!

As you look at your list, let it form onto your consciousness. Who is that person who is doing all those things? What does that person look like? How does that person act?

Billionaire Ed Mylett says that when you die, you go to heaven and meet the person you were destined to become. The person you meet is the best version of you, and his definition of hell is meeting that person and being completely dissimilar. Heaven is meeting that person, looking them in the eye, and recognizing them as a near mirror image of who you were on earth.

Now look again at that list with your best self in mind. Why is going to the Super Bowl important to you? Why is going to Paris with your daughter important to you? What is it about your best self that is important to you?

Once You Know, Map It Out

Put the list away for a day or two and go about your life. Take the garbage out, go to work, eat dinner with your family. Have fun with friends.

Then, a day or so later, look at the list again. Look at what is important to you on that list. What things jump out at you? Maybe getting to Paris is *really* important to you. You are drawn to it for some reason. Why? What does having what you want represent? Security? Freedom?

As you look at your list, ask yourself, *Who is the person who does these things?* Write down who that person is. Write it down where you can review it every month or so. Keep it with you if you can.

Your goal is to start *being* the person who is living the life that your list represents. You may not have a million dollars yet. But how does a person with a million dollars *act*? How are they *being*? How are *you* being?

Multimillionaire real estate developer Manny Khoshbin used this approach when he was sixteen. He literally drew a picture of his home, the trees and cars that were outside of his home, and his wife. Thirty years later he woke up and realized that he was living the life that he drew out on that paper decades before—right down to the look of his wife.[22]

Why?

I believe this happens because the subconscious mind will map out ways to get us where we want to be. But the reverse is true as well: If you think negative thoughts, your subconscious mind will map out ways to get to that negative end. If we focus on the negative impact racism has on our lives, we might unwittingly bring on more of those negative impacts. If, on the other hand, we choose to focus on the positives in our lives, we might see more opportunity come our way.

Perhaps you think that the last paragraph is a little New Age. I get it! But what if I'm right? What if there is something to this approach? What if your subconscious steers you toward decisions and opportunities so that you end up in the life of your dreams?

You need to know where you are going if you want to find the path there. So write it out. Think about where you want to be in five years. Determine to make decisions that will get you closer to where you want to be. You will notice that opportunities will arise.

And that's what I found myself doing in 2016 and 2017. I had to recalibrate. I had the misfortune of a health scare, which led to me spending time with myself. The noise of my life quieted down and I could hear the question, *Is this what you want?* and saw that I did not really want the quality of life I was living.

Rather than waiting for life to knock you down, take some time off and look at where you are, what you truly want, and whether making some changes can get you where you want to be. Decide right now that you want to live your best life *today*. The first step to doing this is being conscious of where you are and where you want to go.

CHAPTER TEN

Be Intentional: Do the Things That Get You Where You Want to Go

"YOU HAVE AN ANSWER for everything," my mother often told me growing up. I don't think she meant that as a compliment. That common refrain was often followed by, "You should be a lawyer." And again, I'm not certain that was supposed to be a compliment either. It was her way of saying, *If you're going to talk back to me all the time and have an answer for every little thing I say, you might as well make a career out of it.*

The more I provided excuses or reasons why things around me were the way they were, the more I heard "You should be a lawyer."

And now, forty years later, I'm sitting at my desk in my law office typing these words before I start my day in my twenty-second year as a lawyer. Although I love what I do, there are certainly days when I wonder whether I have this

your intended destination? We don't travel that way—yet that is how we live our lives: reacting to conditions rather than intentionally moving toward a goal. Living with your North Star in front of you and making decisions based on it will get you to where you are going as opposed to wandering in the wilderness.

Just Do It Now

Have you ever said to yourself, *I'll be happy when I have a million dollars?* Or, *I'll be happy when I'm married?* Or, *I'll be happy when I buy a certain car? I'll be happy when I meet the man of my dreams?* Let me ask you: Why do you need to wait on a million dollars to be happy? Why do you need to wait on a car or another person to be happy? Why do you need to wait to be happy? What about this:

I'll be happy when I have a million dollars.

I'll be happy when I'm married.

I'll be happy when I buy that car.

I'll be happy when I find my partner.

You can ultimately just *decide to be happy*. Obviously, a million dollars gives you a certain level of comfort and freedom. But will it really satisfy you? Once you have a million dollars, you'll likely be around other people who have even more money. So what do you do? You move the goal: *I'll be happy when I have two million dollars.* You end up chasing more money for greater satisfaction that never arrives.

Becoming more intentional about what you're doing is a surefire way to move closer to your North Star no matter how far away it seems. For example, if you're having trouble paying the gas bill, figure out why and make moves to change that reality. Look for strategies to earn, save, or find the money you need to get that bill paid every month.

There comes a time when we need to look at our decisions and take responsibility for areas of our lives, such as our finances. Rather than blaming our financial insecurity on racism, the government, our parents, our neighborhood, our color, or our sex, we can look at our decisions and how those decisions have impacted our financial insecurity. Maybe our race, sex, neighborhood, or parents impacted our financial insecurity too, but as an adult, what role do our decisions have on where we currently sit? Yes, my parents' decisions impacted me when I was fourteen years old, but what decisions do I make that impact my finances at thirty? Once we recognize that our parents, community, friends, and media impact our conditioning and decision-making, and then turn inward to examine that, we can focus on making decisions to create different outcomes and change our lives.

Not terribly long ago, my business owed $75,000 to the IRS. At the same time, our credit cards had balances of over $30,000. I thought I had worked very hard to get both of those balances down. Credit card debt has burdened me my entire life. It started in college when a credit card with an available credit limit of $500 magically appeared in the mail. I got a bunch of horrible pizza at five dollars apiece and by the end of my freshman year defaulted on a credit card with a $500 balance. My credit woes grew while I was in law school—spending money I didn't have on beer, bars, and burritos. And it continued to grow after school—and as I was in my thirties and forties. I continued to spend and not pay the balances back, and I got used to having tens of thousands of dollars in credit card debt.

There was not a grand conspiracy against me. *I was spending too much money.*

Then one day as I was driving to work, I heard Lisa Nichols on Lewis Howes's *School of Greatness* podcast, and I said *enough*. I remember thinking to myself that the one constant over decades of accumulated debt was *me*. It was my decision-making that got me to the space where I was anchored with over $30,000 in credit card debt and $75,000 in IRS business debt.

I was able to justify bad debt. I started my law firm. We had just moved to the suburbs and bought our home in a great school district with a nice backyard and basement and attached garage that we were going to raise our children in. We had just purchased our American Dream. But it cost us more money than we anticipated, and more money was going out every month than was coming in. I woke up every morning at 3:24 a.m., my brain racing to figure out where I could raise money to pay the mortgage. Could I hold off selling stock? How much further into our savings did I have to dip? I justified the IRS debt because it was either pay the federal government the tax I owed or pay the mortgage. Unfortunately, the tax I owed didn't just disappear. It, like the credit card debt, kept increasing. The government didn't forget the bill I had.

At year five, business revenue grew. We could afford to pay the mortgage, pay ourselves back, and live without worrying about monthly bills. We still had to splurge on extracurriculars—like kids' sports—but I wasn't getting up in the middle of the night worried about the mortgage.

But once we earned relative financial peace, neither the IRS debt nor credit card debt decreased. I paid the minimum on both and with interest, but both debts kept increasing. I started getting up at 3:24 again, not because I was worried about the mortgage but because I was worried about why these numbers were not going down. What was I doing wrong?

That's when I heard Lisa Nichols talk about her life—and it changed my life. As she emphasized that it was *her decisions* that put her in that position, it hit me.

My decisions had put me where I was. It wasn't the mortgage; it was the decision to buy more house than we could afford a few months after starting a new business. We had chosen to double our expenses at a time when my income was cut in half. *That was my decision.* My race had nothing to do with that decision. The consequence of that decision was waking up every night struggling to figure out how the mortgage would be paid, stressing out at the office about my firm's revenue, and holding on to a significant amount of credit card debt. These were the consequences of the decision we made to buy *that* house in *that* suburb at *that* time. And the consequences from *that* decision reverberated in our lives for years.

I do not regret making that decision at all. We built a great life because of that decision. Having to fight, struggle, and sacrifice was something we learned and grew from. The biggest growth was learning that my unconscious decision-making put me in that predicament. It was my decisions—not the mortgage company—that woke me up every morning. Ironically, learning that my decisions created those consequences gave me freedom. It gave me freedom because I learned if I wanted a different result, I could choose differently. If I wanted a different life where I wasn't in staggering debt, I could choose to do things differently so I wouldn't continue to live in staggering debt.

I decided to create new habits that would help me become debt-free. Rather than just resolving not to spend money on my credit card—a resolution that went out the window as soon as the furnace broke—I resolved to get up every morning and *create a habit to get myself out of debt.*

I already had a habit of checking my bank account to calculate whether I had enough money to cover checks I'd written. However, this was a fear-based habit. So I decided I would go on offense instead. Each morning, I would go into the account and pay $33.33 on my credit card. In this way, by every third day, I had repaid $100; every week, $233.33; and every month, $1,000. Sometimes, if I could afford it, I would pay $50 or $100. If things were especially tight, I might pay as little as five dollars. But every single day, I made a payment.

Like clockwork, the balances started coming down. One card had had a balance of $14,000 for several years and it looked weird when that balance fell below $10,000. Then it fell below $7,500. As it got close to $5,000, I paid more to get it under that amount. It almost became fun. And what was great is that I was actually doing what I said I wanted to do. I decided to get out of this debt, and watching the debt decrease based on my consistent action gave me confidence. And one day that $30,000 in debt went down to 10 percent of the credit limit. And then that 10 percent of credit limit went down to zero balance. I went from not ever being able to get myself out of debt to deciding to do something different, building a habit around that decision, continuously doing that thing so it became a habit, and in two years—one little step at a time—we were out of credit card debt.

I did the same thing with the federal and state tax debts. I hired a lawyer to keep myself out of trouble as I paid the debts down. Then for the state debt, I automated payments. The state gets paid before I get paid—in that way the debt did not continue to increase. And then, just like the credit card debt, every week, I'd write a check. And that balance would continue to come down. If I got a spike in revenue, the check would be bigger. If not, it would be as little as $100. I kept meticulous track of what was owed and what had been paid. I had a folder of so much paper from the Illinois Department of Revenue and IRS on what was owed, it weighed down my briefcase. But slowly that paper would be tossed because the payments were being made. The conversations with the Illinois Department of Revenue became easier because they saw I was current and that payments on the balance were being paid.

The same thing happened with the Feds. I consulted with my attorney, and when a fee would come in, I'd devote 100 percent of it to back taxes. Twenty thousand here; $10,000 there. If I couldn't spare $10,000, I'd get a check for $5,000 out. When I couldn't spare $5,000, I'd send a check for $2,000. The goal was to get the check out.

Was it fun? No. I'd rather use $20,000 on something for my family or invest it in the stock market. I'm not a club guy, but spending that money in the club would probably have been a hell of a lot more fun than sending it to the federal government. But I decided to get myself out of debt. And I committed to the decision. I decided that my future me would be better positioned by sending the check to the Feds rather than going to a club or investing it in Microsoft or taking Amy and the kids to Florida.

I wanted to be debt-free. I wanted to be a business owner that wasn't beholden to the government for back taxes anymore.

I wanted the consequence of sending the check to the government more than I wanted the consequence of *not* sending the check to the government.

I wanted future me to be in the position he was in because I sent the check to the government.

I decided to start *being* future me when I drove down the highway with Lisa Nichols ringing in my ears. Future me paid his taxes. Future me did not have credit card debt. Being future me and making decisions as future me *for* future me grew me into future me.

Similar to how my mother's refrain of "You have an answer for everything" put me on the path to becoming a lawyer, Lisa

Nichols's instruction on the impact her decisions had on her life woke me up to what I was unconsciously doing. If the goal was to eliminate this debt, I had to stop finding ways to justify having debt and decide to do things to pay it off.

When I made the decision to do this, I did not have the income to support paying down over $105,000 in debt in under two years. I didn't foresee or anticipate or extrapolate that I had extra money to pay down these debts. I just started paying. Here's the wild thing: after I made the decision to pay down these debts first, the money to pay them started flowing more easily. The business revenue significantly increased. It was almost like once I decided to do it, it started happening.

Make Your Decisions and Stick It Out

Decisions create consequences. People who work out regularly understand the importance of deciding to do something and doing it. It's not going to the gym today that creates the future you, but the decision and commitment to go three or four times a week for months. It's going to the gym when you don't want to, knowing that you'll feel accomplished once you do. You keep doing it and you keep doing it and one day you look up and see the body in the mirror that you worked so hard to get.

But the single decision to do it *today* is important.

That single decision to do it today creates momentum for tomorrow. The single decision to do it today builds a habit so you're more likely to do it tomorrow. The single decision to do it today gives you confidence that it can be done—especially on days you don't want to.

THAT SINGLE DECISION TO DO IT TODAY CREATES MOMENTUM FOR TOMORROW.

And the more you go, the more opportunities are created. At first you go to the gym and work on things on your own. At the gym you start seeing the same people and those people push you to go to a fitness class. And you meet more people who suggest routines. And then you decide to invest in a trainer who gets you to the next level in your fitness. And then you find yourself with more people who are fit; getting up to meet with that trainer once a week makes it more likely that you'll work out more on your own.

The decision to do one thing consistently leads to opportunities for growth.

Think about school. The decision to invest in education leads to growth. You go to school and learn concepts in sixth grade. You keep going and keep going and keep going and learn and learn and learn and you find yourself in ninth grade learning new things because you built on concepts you learned three years before in sixth grade.

But if you don't commit to learn something in sixth grade, it will be that much more difficult to learn more advanced concepts in ninth grade. And the opportunities you gain from knowing those advanced concepts in ninth grade won't materialize for you. All because you did not commit to doing the work before.

Here I am today, working on this book—*as I write these words*—because future me is a published author. I am doing things today for future me.

The decision *not* to commit to learning affects your future ability and opportunity.

The decision *not* to commit to putting away five dollars a day rather than buying Starbucks affects your future self because you don't have $1,825 in your savings account at the end of the year.

The decision *not* to pay debt had me overwhelmed by having to pay off $105,000 in debt.

The decision to move forward is easier when you are moving toward your North Star. It's easier to get up every morning and do something to move you toward the North Star when it's something you want. If you want to go to Paris and need $20,000 to do it, it's easier to forgo that Starbucks coffee or dinner or two extra cocktails when you actively decide to save that money, watch the money grow, and visualize yourself in Paris. But that's why your North Star is so important. Because if it's not important to you, you'll opt for Starbucks or you'll opt for the snooze button five times, or you'll opt for something other than what you're working toward.

Doing that thing leaves you confident you can do it. You can pay your tax; you can save money for an awesome trip to Florida; you can gain the physique you want; you can write that book. Making the decision to intentionally work toward a goal and seeing progress in reaching those goals builds your confidence to create and work toward bigger goals. Gaining those bigger goals will only enhance your life. Achieving the goals creates more opportunity, which creates bigger goals, creating greater opportunity. Your life momentum will feed itself.

Commit to your North Star right now. Make one small decision to do something in furtherance of your North Star *right now*. Seriously, I'll stop writing so you can stop reading and do something *right now*!

Congratulations! You Did That Thing!

AWESOME! You did something to move intentionally toward your goal.

If you did not, do *not* turn the page, do *not* pass GO and collect $200. Do one thing that gets you closer to future you.

If you did do that thing, stop reading and do something else!

(SERIOUSLY!)

Building Habits That Reflect Your Goals

AWESOME! You did at least two things to move intentionally toward your goals.

Now think about the habit you will need to build to get you toward your goals.

Do your habits reflect your goals? I heard former Ohio State University football coach Urban Meyer ask this once on the *School of Greatness,*[23] so I wrote it down and framed it, and it sits in my office as a reminder.

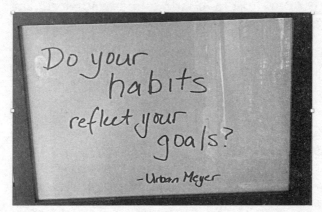

Before I got out of debt, I had this habit of checking my bank account every day. The purpose was to make sure I had money and estimate when money would flow out of my account so new checks would be covered. Rather than creating a whole new habit, I used that habit of logging into my account every morning to log in and make a credit card payment every morning. I built my habit to pay down debt every morning out of an old habit.

Building a habit to get me to my North Star from an old habit made it stickier—because I was already doing it.

Now it's your turn: evaluate your current habits and see where you can build on one that gets you closer to your North Star. What if you're not sure what your habits are? Do this by mindfully going through your day. Use your shower as an example—you often wash your body parts in the same order daily without thinking about it. How do your unconscious daily habits with your family, with your work, with your free time get you closer to or farther from your North Star?

I'll stop writing so you can do that...

Enjoy the Cake Too!

FIRST, GIVE YOURSELF a high five for getting here and doing the small things that get you closer to your goal. Acknowledge the work you are doing. Don't only focus on the goal, focus on the one tiny step you took today that got your closer.

One day—hell, many days—you're not going to want to do that one tiny thing. And you know what—some days that's okay. It's okay to eat the birthday cake. Life is not to be lived without cake. Eat the cake!

But the next day, put the running shoes back on and get out and run even if it's less than what you typically do.

And on the next day you don't want to take the action toward your goal, force yourself to do it, even if you do less than what you typically do—I promise you'll feel better once it's done.

CHAPTER ELEVEN

Let the Past Be

HAVE YOU EVER woken up hungover after a few too many? It's a miserable feeling, often made worse by shame and embarrassment over what you may have said or done the night before. And then you pray. *Dear God, If you get me through this, I'll never drink again!*

Have you ever been there? You limp to the couch to figure out what essential things you can attempt to do, like turning on the television (low volume!) and crawling to the fridge to get some Sprite.

Most of us have been on that couch, in misery, thinking about all those things we thought were great ideas, having engaged in more mischief and mayhem than bad karaoke. And we sit there and wallow in our embarrassment made worse by the physical effects of the hangover. The constant refrain of "Did I really say that?" goes through our head. And eventually, as the day moves on and the hangover starts to dissipate—thank God for McDonald's!—that embarrassment also starts to wane.

Somewhere between that horrible hangover and the following weekend, *you let the past go.* You drop all the stories you were telling about yourself and just let it be. You move forward with your life: going to work, talking to friends, hanging out with your family. You just let the past *be.*

So much so that the next weekend, you're feeling great! You tip back another drink and find yourself talking with the same person you thought you offended last weekend.

Somewhere between that horrible hangover and the following weekend, you let the past go.

That's what we have to do in life; we have to let the past be. We have a choice on whether we want to drop the past stories about our limitations because of slavery, because we never got reparations, because this nation was built on our free labor, because they won't allow me to get an education, because I was born poor, because my hair is too kinky, because I'm too dark-skinned, because I'm too light-skinned, because I'm not smart, because I'm not attractive, because I'm too fat, because I'm too skinny.

We carry around all this baggage in our mental backpack for our lifetime without realizing it. Nobody is saying to forget and act like these past atrocities never happened. What we're saying is not to allow these past atrocities to affect today's decision-making. To do that breathes new life into the atrocities. To allow slavery to affect a decision you make today breathes new life into slavery. To allow segregation to affect a decision you make today breathes new life into segregation.

We have been conditioned by our parents, friends, communities, schools, churches, and media to believe we are less than, and that conditioning, that belief that we're less than, makes decisions for us. That's why we need to be aware of that conditioning. Our awareness of our conditioning will allow us to control our mindset, which affects our response. When we consider where we want to go and make decisions based on that rather than our past experience, we can start knocking out goals.

Refusing to let the past control the present can require us to actively work against a lifetime of conditioning, which operates a bit like muscle memory.

Consider driving to a place you've never been. Maybe you consult a map and figure out the best route to get to your location. You may have written directions with you. You're on high alert looking for streets and landmarks to get you where you're going That first time—maybe even the first few times—you are very intentional about taking the correct route to get there.

But then think about driving yourself somewhere you have been hundreds of times, like work. Do you even consider where you're going? Or do you just get in the car and arrive at your destination? Because your route has been driven so many times, you don't even think about where you're going and you arrive there, almost magically.

That is an example of conditioning and its potential dangers. When a certain stimulus or thought comes in, you don't even think of the response because your brain has a conditioned response for that particular thought.

When the thought of investing in yourself by getting an education pops into your head, maybe your conditioned response, fueled by *I am less than,* is to ignore that suggestion because you can't do that. Even thinking about getting an education is silly, because (insert your limiting belief here).

Limiting beliefs are thoughts about yourself and the world you hold to be true, that hold you back or restrict you in some way. Perhaps those limiting beliefs were passed down from your parents, from their parents, from their parents. You get them from peers and the media. Limiting beliefs are based on American society and culture. Because of all of your influences, you may think you are "too old" or "not pretty enough" or "not smart enough" to take a certain path—*a path you want to take.* This can be worse in the Black community because American society restricted us legally and socially for centuries. There was a time we were not allowed to get an education. So even thinking about getting an education was silly because it wasn't possible.

Seventy years ago, it was much more difficult to become a lawyer. Few of us had the educational opportunity before college to prepare for it. Even if we had the ability and education to get into college, we'd have to find a college that would accept us. On June 11, 1963, two—*two!*—black students named Vivian Malone and James A. Hood showed up for summer school at the University of Alabama when Alabama governor George Wallace stood in the doorway blocking the threshold to education.[24]

Image from AP

Governor George Wallace, who famously said, "Segregation now, segregation tomorrow, segregation forever," stood in the doorway preventing Black students the opportunity to get an education that white students routinely received and took for granted. This wasn't some random dude off the street; *this was the governor*. The governor leads a state and speaks for its people. The state of Alabama gave direction: white Alabamans, it's okay to deny Black people civil rights and something as simple as the opportunity to receive an education. Black Alabamans: don't you dare even consider thinking about getting an education.

We have more choices now than past generations. We now have the opportunity to apply for and get into college without state governors blocking our entrance to the doors of higher education and opportunity. State government no longer stands at the door to educational opportunity. But our conditioning now stands at the door where George Wallace stood. Are we distracted by the mess of messaging tying us down to where we currently are—or do we make decisions that put us on the path for growth?

We do not suffer from the same systemic racism our grandparents suffered from. George Wallace, thankfully, was wrong. Segregation is dead. Redlining is illegal. We can get any job we want. We can live anywhere we can afford to live.

However, for those who say segregation is alive and well, I ask you whether the government truly keeps you where you live. Does the governor of your state publicly disenfranchise you because of your race? Does the governor block your entrance to the doors of a public university?

De facto segregation exists today. But how much of

today's de facto segregation is because of our past conditioning? We keep ourselves in neighborhoods with underperforming schools. There is a way out of that neighborhood. There is a path forward toward a better job. There is a path forward toward better schools.

The government is not going to help you out of bad circumstances. We can argue about whether the government should help—given its responsibility and complicity in putting us there. But debating whether it should help will not make that help come any faster, if it all. Accept that we're on our own and make decisions that will help our children take steps forward in the privilege race rather than allowing our decisions to keep our children at the starting line.

Although we should remember the past and what our grandparents had to do to attend a public university, we also have to let it go and not carry around those burdens day in and day out. We can't allow past humiliation to put us in an "I can't" mindset. We have a choice to make: we can decide to make decisions to help us find opportunities or to find examples when Blackness is used against us. Both exist. But what mindset best serves us? What mindset, what approach, serves us in getting to goals? What approach best serves George Wallace's end of "segregation now, segregation tomorrow, segregation forever"? Your decisions determine whose world comes into being. Do you want it to be George

Wallace's world? Or do you want it to look more like Martin Luther King Jr.'s where we are judged by the content of our character rather than the color of our skin? When Martin Luther King Jr. said those words in 1963, two months after George Wallace denied Black students the right to a public education, we did not have the same opportunities that we have today. Take advantage of the opportunities we have and use those opportunities to propel you into the future.

Learn Your Conditioning and Focus on the Future

It's Sunday morning at 10 a.m. and I'm sweating, clammy, queasy, and generally feeling hungover. Didn't I say *last time* that the *last time* would be the *last time*?

It's funny how we can easily forget about the past and then fall right back into our same habits. The last time we suffered from that severe hangover—and many times before that—we lay there in bed or on the couch, clammy, sweating, and feeling lousy, and said, "This is the last time!"

Only to be there again.

The hangover example proves that we can forget about the past. That these hangovers occurred regularly in my twenties is clear proof that I have the ability to forget the past. The question is whether I will change my decisions to change my future. I can easily continue with my conditioning. I'm a better dancer when I drink. It's easier for me to talk to women when I drink. Confidence equals a couple of drinks. Isn't that why alcohol has been called liquid courage? All these things we tell ourselves ultimately lead to patterns and habits that do not serve us.

It's great that we can forget about the past. It's not so great when we don't take the opportunity to learn a lesson from it.

FOCUSING ON THE PAST WON'T PROPEL US INTO THE FUTURE WE WANT. FOCUSING ON CENTURIES OF OUR OWN VICTIMHOOD WILL KEEP US VICTIMS. FOCUSING ON OUR CONDITIONING AND BELIEFS, SHINING A LIGHT OR AWARENESS ON OUR CONDITIONING AND BELIEFS AND THEN QUESTIONING WHETHER THOSE BELIEFS SERVE US, CAN HELP BUILD AND CREATE A BETTER FUTURE.

For generations, our political and religious leaders have focused on the past. Our history as slaves, the birth of the Ku Klux Klan, Jim Crow, Black Codes, the GI Bill, redlining are the reasons for where we are today. Although that all may be true, focusing on the past won't propel us into the future we want. Focusing on centuries of our own victimhood will keep us victims. Focusing on our conditioning and beliefs, shining a light or awareness on our conditioning and beliefs and then questioning whether those beliefs serve us, can help build and create a better future.

When I had the belief that I needed alcohol in my system to be charming to women—or have the courage to talk to them—I made that belief true. But, looking back on it, did it serve me? Was it true? Did I make it true? Did I convince myself I was charming after I had a couple of drinks in me? That was the belief I wore. Could I have chosen to wear the "I am charming" belief?

Ultimately, if I don't have the confidence to speak to someone unless I have three drinks in me, what does that say about my confidence? How can I fix that? Does drinking alcohol to gain confidence fix the problem? Or should I work on my self-confidence?

The same way I needed to examine my most basic beliefs about my self-worth, many of us need to do the same thing with our self-worth in American society. Yes, America has told us for centuries we are not enough—we need to stop listening. America has started to provide us opportunities that we should have had centuries ago. Let's grab them. Grab them so the conversation we have at Thanksgiving surrounds gratitude for our abundance rather than thanks for the little we have. Although we are grateful and should be grateful for what we have, we can start living lives where we thrive rather than just survive. That's what we can start working toward when we focus on the future. That's what we can start working toward when we shine awareness on our stories, beliefs, and conditioning and we decide to do something different when what we are doing doesn't serve us.

Racism exists. As I said before, gravity also exists. But we all know that the Wright brothers came along and said, "You know what, let's defy gravity. Build a machine so we can fly!" Fast-forward a hundred years and our planet relies on our ability to defy gravity. Even if you've never flown in an airplane, you rely on flight to get the food you eat from the grocery store or the clothes you wear.

Sadly, racism in America is like gravity: it is going to be there (at least in our lifetimes). The decision on whether we want to defy racism and move forward despite it is ours.

You are where you are today because of the decisions you have made. If you assess where you are today and don't like that place, then honestly assess why you're there. What role do you play in your life?

There comes a time when responsibility for your life—and where you sit today—moves from your parents to you.

There comes a time in your life where your decisions put you where you are. Not your parents'. Not America's failures and institutionalized racism. You.

And if not you, then who?

You get to make the decision on whether you will get an education. You can be seventeen and make that decision. You can be twenty-nine and make that decision. You can be fifty-four and make that decision. But the decision to invest in yourself and get an education is yours. Not your mother's. Not your friend's. Not America's. The decision to invest in your education is yours.

The decision to have a child is yours. Institutionalized racism will not make that decision for you.

Your mother may have helped you make that decision, if this is what you saw your mother do. Your neighborhood—and the people around you—may have helped you make that decision if that is what your neighbors do.

But if that is what your mother did, if that is what your neighbors do, ask yourself: Is it working? Did my mother struggle to make ends meet? How many steps forward in that privilege race do you get to take when you live with a single mother struggling to make ends meet?

Your mother may be a great, hardworking woman. Perhaps your mother sacrificed everything she had to put food on your table. The issue is not whether your mother worked hard and sacrificed; the issue is whether she is thriving and whether you can make different decisions to put you in a better position to thrive. Are there decisions that will get me from survive to thrive? Are there decisions I can make that will give me more income?

This applies to everyone—me included. Do you make $100,000 a year? Great! What decisions can you make to make $200,000 a year—if that is what you want? We don't have to accept what our parents accepted. We don't have to accept what our grandparents accepted. There is so much more opportunity for us today—we should take advantage of it.

My good fortune is that my parents asked themselves this question back in 1978. What can we do to give our children a chance at a better life? What can we do to thrive rather than just survive? If I want more—how can I go out and get it? That is when they decided to move to Elmhurst.

Two hundred years ago, people who lived in population centers near rivers had a higher standard of living because of the ease in which goods could get to them. To get that standard of living, people had to move to towns near the river to get easier access to these goods. The river was a resource and towns on rivers had better access to these resources.

Assuming education is the key to prosperity—I think it is the most viable way to prosperity (but certainly not the only)—we can return to that approach and move to where the resources are. If your community does not have access to a good education that will propel your children to college, if you want your children to go to college, you can intentionally find housing in a town with an excellent school district. Move to where the resources are.

Yes, we should be squeaky wheels about the inequities in school funding. But ultimately, if the elected representatives doling out those resources aren't listening, what does that do for your child's education today? If you know districts X, Y, and Z have these resources, then find a way to get into districts X, Y, or Z.

The best way to manage this is making the decision at eighteen rather than twenty-eight. By deciding "my children are going to go to school in one of these school districts" at eighteen, you'll have more opportunity to build the resources to be able to make that happen before you have children. Is this a lot to put on an eighteen-year-old? It is. However, the alternative, not thinking about these things and bringing a child into the world, is also a lot. A decision to invest today will make that circumstance come true tomorrow.

The person who decides to have children at thirty, after twelve years of investment, will find it easier to get to that school district than someone making the same decision at twenty-nine with a ten-year-old and one year of investment. Most people who have a child at eighteen are not thinking about getting that child into a great school district. If you're eighteen, you're worried about putting food on the table, affording diapers, formula, and childcare. You are not worried about getting your kid into a good school district.

Because we tend to repeat what we see (in the same way we limit ourselves in the way we tell ourselves we can't do things), I subconsciously invested, moved, and sacrificed, just like my parents had done.

Before you think that my life is the greatest because I have parents who were very intentional on putting my sister and me into a great position to succeed, know that it was not all sunshine and rainbows. My family life—my mother, father, and sister—was not a Norman Rockwell painting.

I say this because you need to know it. You deserve to know it. I'm getting on a soapbox and preaching how we can change our lives through shifting mindsets and making better decisions, but you should know where my difficulties are. I don't want to lord over you like I have it all figured out when many days I'm in the weeds too. If I have a significant area of my life that doesn't look the way I want it to look—you should know it's there.

I have great fortune in my family in that my parents stayed married until I graduated college and worked their asses off providing us the opportunity to take sixteen steps forward in the privilege race. They also showed us how hard work pays dividends. Sure, they told us to work hard, but we do what we see. I was fortunate to see that hard work.

But I also get stuck in some pretty sad patterns that were likely developed decades ago. I don't talk to my father. We text on birthdays to make certain we are still alive. But he is not present in my life. My children don't know him—have never met him. I remember the last time I saw him—my sister was moving to California—and that was perhaps 2013.

Growing up, I didn't know my father's father. My family ignored that fact—much like how my children don't know my father and that fact is largely ignored.

This all scares me to death. I have accepted the fact that I won't have much of a relationship with my father. I fear that I have accepted this series of decisions as fate. But I'm really scared of abandoning my son because that is what I know. I'm afraid of not being around for my children. I'm afraid of not being around for him when he needs me as an adult.

Maybe my parents felt abandoned by their families. Maybe that 1970s interracial marriage put them on a trajectory away from their families that I can't or didn't realize. I know my father's decisions caused ripples within his family: his decision to marry a white woman and move to a predominantly white suburb were not taken well.

My father is not around and I can't really speak to why.

I can't get past the hurt attached to the void and I have difficulty acknowledging my role in it. I know I play a role. I know I bear some blame, but again, I can't figure it out. It's blocked. Or maybe I keep it blocked to focus on other things: building my law practice, investing money to fund the lifestyle I desire, writing this book, being a father and husband, being a valued member of the village we've built around us, building awareness of my conditioning, and building new habits to make me a better version of myself.

I tell myself all the time that I'm not enough. So I choose to work on that rather than working on the void that is my relationship with my parents. I wonder if I fixed that other thing—the relationship with my parents—would the "I'm not enough" voice in my head go away?

The point of my mini-therapy session on this page is that *it is not easy*. There is messiness in my life—back in 1978 and today. I am still working on a lot of my conditioning and beliefs.

But as I sit here on my soapbox and encourage you on how to live your best life, you have to know that my life is far from perfect. There are a great many places in your life where I want much more of what *you* have.

But that's the key: acknowledging that and going out to get it. Taking ownership of what you have and finding solutions to fixing the things you don't have but want. Once we take ownership of where we are, once we admit and acknowledge that our decisions created the life we are living, then we can focus awareness on areas we want to change and go about taking the strides—by being intentional and making decisions—to change them. It could be as easy as "I want to travel more." Great—decide where you want to go and figure out a way you will get there and do it. Take that first step. After that first step, we take the next.

Moving Past the Paralysis of Our Conditioning

Taking ownership of the good and the bad, finding ways to fix whatever's wrong rather than waiting for someone to save us—these are the things we must do to move past the paralysis of our conditioning. Once we acknowledge that our decisions create the life we live, then we can take the strides necessary to get us where we want to be. This applies to any goal you have, big or small.

Conditioning paralysis applies to our white brothers and sisters, too, but ours is different because society has laid and continues to lay a blanket on us that makes it harder for us to move forward. Institutional racism, the bias we encounter daily when we enter the world, makes it harder for us to succeed, so we throw up our hands and say we can't succeed because we're

Black. We *must* fight back against beliefs that don't serve us.

Oluo's "I have never been able to escape the fact that I am a black woman in a white supremacist country" is true. She is 100 percent correct. When we go out daily with the mindset that the world is against us, we will judge or interpret every look given, word uttered, perceived slight, or smile through that lens.

Your Parents Did the Best with What They Had

I love being a father. I have a mug at home that says "World's #1 Dad!" And I am. I was like "What the heck?!" when I saw a guy in my office with the very same mug. I pointed my finger at him and said "Look, Jim, I don't know where you got that mug, but for the record, *I'm* the world's number one dad. You can be number two, but I'm number one!"

Although I am the world's #1 dad, I mess up quite often in that role. It's my knee-jerk reactions to something my kids do that afterward make me cringe. Many times, I hear myself saying things said to me thirty-five years ago: "Hey, am I the maid?!" "BECAUSE I SAID SO!" "You are not leaving that table until you clean your plate!" These phrases cause an involuntary shiver down my spine when I realize that somehow I became my mother.

NFL running back Adrian Peterson was suspended from

football for one year when allegations that he beat his four-year-old son with a switch became public. During the uproar, we learned that he was beat with a switch when he grew up. Adrian Peterson was doing what was done to him.

And that is what we do as parents. We repeat the patterns of our parents. My parents disciplined me with a belt. "Disciplined" is being gracious in terms of what occurred and the fear I had growing up (especially with those huge 1970s belts). I could hear my father's belt buckle if I was down the street at a friend's house when he took off his belt after work. I couldn't hear my mother call my name, but I heard that belt buckle.

There's a good chance I would've done the same to my children if it weren't for my wife. As a social worker who interacts with abused children, she taught me that physically punishing children is wrong.

I'm grateful for learning that lesson, which has allowed me to break a chain of generational trauma. Although I still jump at times when I hear *my own* belt buckle clink as an adult, I'm grateful that my children won't have to live with that same reaction. My wife assures me that someone somewhere who knows a whole lot more about child development than I do says beating your kids is bad, and I believe her. Besides, discipline doesn't have to be physical to be effective: sometimes it seems like my kids suffer more when their phones are taken away than I ever did from a beating.

When I started looking at my unconscious beliefs, my first thought was, *Damn, my parents messed me up!* Then I dug a little deeper and noticed that they were doing their best with what they had. Just like my intention is not screwing up my children, that doesn't mean I'm not passing down unconscious beliefs that will not serve them. I know I am! Because *I* still struggle with unconscious beliefs. How am I modeling those beliefs without being conscious of them?

I realize how very fortunate I am to have had two parents who stayed together—which was not easy for them—and worked hard and climbed the economic ladder. Seeing my parents do that, work hard and build, build, build, conditioned me to do the same.

There are the negative habits built by conditioning. Smoking, drug use, problematic drinking, failure to exercise, poor diet, yelling at your spouse, to name a few.

Even some "good" things can be negative, like playing it safe or "being responsible." As we strive for more, our governors keep us in a safe zone, keep us where we won't fail. We won't apply for that job, because we already have a good one and don't want to mess anything up. But getting that other job means more work, more money, more responsibility, and more future opportunity, all great things, but our governor will kick in, slowing us down to where we feel safe.

The governor I'm talking about is not a political leader of a state, but the "device automatically regulating the supply of fuel, steam, or water to a machine, ensuring uniform motion or limiting speed."[25]

We all have governors built into our brains and bodies meant to keep us safe. This can be a good thing, but it also keeps us on the ground when we could be flying. These governors are passed down generationally as conditioning. My mother always said "Money doesn't grow on trees" to keep us in a lack mentality when it came to money. Apparently, my grandmother said that all the time. So now when I say that to my children, they downshift from trying to go for something that may cost a little more and require more of an abundance mindset. A governor is put in place because a negative relationship with money was built by my great-grandmother with her child during the Great Depression that still affects my children ninety years later.

That's conditioning.

It's nobody's fault. My grandmother saying "money doesn't grow on trees" to my mother was her imparting what she believed to be an important lesson. It just may not have been the right one. Your grandmother's lesson passed down decades ago may be far less relevant in the present. It could be the lesson that keeps you working a job you don't want rather than going for the career you do.

Do I want to carry around the belief that I can't do something? Or that I'm fragile? Or that I am not enough? Or that my grandchildren won't know me?

Or do I want something different?

We can choose to do something different than what our parents did. We can choose better relationships with money, the opposite sex, food, drugs and alcohol, exercise, other races, *ourselves*, than our parents modeled for us. To do this, we must be aware of our conditioning. As children, we did not control the grooves being formed in our brains.

Just like that path in the woods that you walked, your brain forms grooves or paths over time from learned reactions to stimulus. For years others before you walked in that forest and a pathway was created to get through the forest. The same thing happens in your brain. For years you were taught to react to certain stimuli. You were taught to react the same way your parents were taught and as their parents were taught.

It takes some courage to get off that forest path and go in a different direction. But by doing that, you're likely to find something that hasn't been seen or noticed in that forest, because you may be the first person to walk that way. You may find something valuable or find a great little spot nobody knows about. You would never have known about that great tree if you didn't get off the path.

Our past experiences with racism put us on the path

where we are not enough. We walk these paths that tell us we can't afford an education. We walk these paths telling us to play it safe in a job that is beneath us. We play it safe by staying with partners who don't treat us the way we want to be treated. We play it safe by doing what our parents did. Even if we see the dysfunction on our path, we'll continue to walk it.

It Is Time to Choose

The way we defeat the legacy of racism is getting off the path we've been on for centuries.

Today you have choices to make.

Do you want to continue where you are, or do you want to do something different?

Do you want to carry your parents' grievances about racism, or do you want to do something different?

Do you want to play it safe in life, or do you want to thrive?

The path you know will always be there for you. The thing about that path is you already know where it goes. There are no promises that getting off the path you know will work out. But getting off the path you know will show you things you have yet to experience, places you have yet to see, new tastes for things you have never tasted. Isn't experiencing life, truly delighting in what life has to offer, what thriving is all about?

Don't trust me. Trust yourself: *Get off the path!*

CHAPTER TWELVE

I Can Change My Circumstances

IT WAS DECEMBER 2001. I was cold and alone and abandoned, sitting on the floor of my father's townhouse. He had one of those really small loveseats, and I used that to lean on. I remember wanting to lie down and look at the ceiling, but the loveseat was too small. I wasn't crying, but I needed to. Although I wasn't particularly close to my father anymore, I needed someplace to go and just be alone. To think. Or not to think. To let time pass. Or let it stop. To just be. Or not be at all. The house was dark; so was I.

My fiancée had just broken up with me.

I had this picture of how life was going to turn out. My fiancée was a doctor and would work as an anesthesiologist. I would work as a lawyer. We would move back to my hometown, buy a big house, have a couple of kids and a dog, have a great social life with my high school and college friends, maybe run for mayor of my hometown, and live happily ever after.

Yet I found myself here. So far away from the dream of the white-picket fence. The dream was gone—dissipated like steam from a hot bath—while I frantically fought to keep it. There were emails, telephone calls, hysterical messages to her relatives and friends as I tried to get her to see it differently, tried to get her back to live my dream.

Yet it was not only my dream that disappeared into thin air; my self-esteem left with it. I had value because *she loved me, and her love told the world I had value.* And when she left to follow her path—her dream—my value left with her.

I had walked into the relationship with my former fiancée with unresolved issues of abandonment; the relationship's end led to me losing myself to alcohol and the party rather than taking a hard look at my feelings. And right when I thought the alcohol intake couldn't go higher, it did. I drank to escape my life and disappointment in myself. I was alone. I drank to warm up, even if it was just for those moments with glass in hand. The parties were loud enough to get lost in and not think. And because the glass warmed me up, I had it in my hand more and more and more. My life started to unravel. I pushed away my friends, sought self-esteem in random hookups, and started to self-destruct.

It was on the floor of my father's house that I decided enough was enough. I didn't want to live this way. I couldn't live like this. I didn't want to undo my life.

If I'm being honest, the anger I had against my former fiancée fueled me. I used that anger as motivation. The same seething fury, that scorned rage, that led me to self-destruct got me up in the morning and drove me to work. My heart pumped that anger throughout my body as I worked late nights. That anger drove a half-assed reinvention. I was able to clean myself up, move to a new apartment, work, and socialize without as much chaos in my wake. I didn't work on my feelings of abandonment and betrayal, but at least I doused the torch I had taken to my life.

I was twenty-seven at the time and I didn't have the tools I have now, or the awareness. I didn't realize that I had been escaping from years of abandonment. Growing up, for all that my parents provided—which was a lot—they did not provide *themselves*. They believed their role was to give us the opportunity that education provided and they worked their asses off to provide that. But the trade-off was that they didn't share themselves, leading me to feel a sense of loss.

Over the years, I used my friends' families as my own. I integrated myself into their families and became the adopted brother or cousin. As I aged, I found a different set of people I could hang out with and feel the comradery of family. As I started going to bars and clubs, I hung out and saw the same people on the circuit and they became a bit of a family. I probably migrated toward the ones, like me, who searched for belonging or identity through the group. The club culture isn't terribly healthy. Looking back, I had a great time; but living a life of pure hedonism, for me at least, was pretty empty. Even the friends I made back then, when we get together today, reminiscence about glory days rather than lessons learned.

Maybe my job isn't to tell them the lesson learned: that I was running from abandonment and that our relationships filled me with a sense of community. That I didn't trust myself or love myself or find myself worthy of love, so I ran to alcohol and the party as a way to fill me up. I was yearning for and seeking a sense of community, a family, a place where I belonged. However, even with people around, I was always alone. The music always eventually stopped. When I left the party, I was completely empty.

As I continued to run from myself—my sense of abandonment with a failed engagement providing yet more proof of my faults—I didn't have any wisdom about why I did the things I did. I just did them. In acting out, I didn't realize I was *re*acting.

I was fortunate, however, because somewhere deep inside I knew I wasn't happy. I knew something was wrong. I could not put a finger on exactly what was wrong and what I was running from, but I knew I had put myself on my father's floor cold and alone. I knew that nobody was coming to save me and that I had to pull myself out of it. I could not rely on my parents as they were dealing with their own issues. It wasn't my friends' job to do it for me. *I* had to do it for *me*. And if I wanted more, I had to find it and work for it. I accepted that my decisions put me on that floor in that dark moment. It wasn't my parents' fault anymore. It wasn't my former fiancée's fault.

At that time, my friends were starting to settle down. Two of my best friends were married and starting to have kids; other friends were starting to leverage their careers into earning and saving enough money to invest and buy homes. I was still leveraging my career to attempt to woo women with the "I'm a lawyer" line while buying booze. I wanted something different. So I started doing something different. I moved toward the goal of investing in myself through my career.

It wasn't all in one day. There was no grand epiphany that happened leading me to restart my life the next day and everything was great. I was still destructive. I was still drinking to excess, trying to impress others by feeding lines about my being the guy I actually could be one day rather than working to be that guy. But even though I was still in the party environment, still doing the destructive things, I did those things less and started taking myself more seriously. I found a great job that centered me as an attorney. People started coming into my life who were doing the same things, but differently. There was time for focus along with time for play. And the play was slightly different. A meal with a drink and great conversation at home. A relaxing Sunday brunch rather than a raging alcohol-fueled Sunday Funday.

I started making decisions that moved me toward the man I wanted to be. I wanted to own a condominium, so I started making investments in myself—by saving and working and cutting spending where I could—to make that happen. Being a lawyer stopped being a line at a bar and started being me. And that led to opportunities to live the life I dreamed of. It got me off my father's floor feeling sorry for myself and got me doing things. A thing here, something there, that over time put me in position to be the person I wanted to be.

I remember buying my first home. It was a wonderful condominium on the third floor of a three-story walk up. It was a 2,000-square-foot, two-bedroom, two-bath with vaulted ceilings in the living room. That living room also had a loft area I used as an office. It was awesome. After I moved in, I remember lying on the floor of that lofted office space. I remember looking at the wall thinking: *This is my wall. I earned this wall.* I lay on *my floor* and thought about lying on my father's floor three years earlier thinking about how bad my life was, all the value I didn't have. And almost like magic, here I was in my own space amazed at how far away that cold night felt.

It's funny how you think you get to the peak of a

mountain and after celebrating for a while, the clouds clear and it turns out there is another mountain for you to climb. That moment on that floor in that lofted office was not quite twenty years ago. Since then it hasn't been smooth sailing. There have been sleepless nights because of medical, financial, career, family, and relationship issues. There have been financial crises, a kidney transplant, a pulmonary embolism, significant IRS debt, the shutdown of an employer, COVID.

You know what? Each time one of those things happened, an opportunity to grow emerged. Do you want something different? Then do something different.

Do Your Habits Reflect Your Goals?

When I picked myself off of my father's floor, I certainly wasn't thinking *Brian, do your habits reflect your goals?* I was feeling sorry for myself, empty because of the emptiness surrounding me. My self-esteem was determined by the value someone else placed on a pickup line. But as I sat on my father's floor, there was this dim recognition that all of the value I placed on myself was based on what I thought others thought about me. I had value because of what others thought about my engagement. I had value because of what people could believe about my being *a lawyer*. I had value because of my circle of friends. I didn't trust or believe that I was worthy;

I had value when others thought I had value.

There was this voice, however faint, telling me things weren't right. There was this voice, however faint, telling me I am better than this. There was this voice, however faint, telling me I deserved more. And rather than be distracted by the noise of the party, I started to listen.

That voice, my inner Rocky Balboa, told me it was time to get up.

Stay Fighting

As I mentioned earlier, Rocky Balboa is my hero. In the boxing ring, Rocky was hit hard by Apollo Creed yet always got back up. Rocky didn't just pop back up, Rocky *fought* to get back up. It would have been easier—maybe even sensible—to stay down.

Rocky has always resonated with me. His strength wasn't how hard he could punch; his strength wasn't not falling; his strength was no matter how hard he got hit—by life or by Apollo or Clubber Lang or Ivan Drago or cancer—he always got up. He always kept fighting. The goal wasn't necessarily to win; the goal was to get up and keep moving forward. One step at a time.

Rocky was proactive. He understood he was going to fall. He accepted falling. But he didn't accept not getting up.

That's all this book asks of you: to start answering your life's bell. If you've wandered through life in the way I wandered—the way most of us wander—shake the cobwebs off, find what you want, and go out and get it.

We do that by living fearlessly. We do that by accepting we will fall. Just like when you learned how to ride a bicycle, failure is inevitable. But if you want to learn how to ride a bike, it's getting up after you scraped your knee and getting back on that seat and trying again. You were Rocky Balboa then. You can be Rocky Balboa now.

Building the Habits That Matter

We do that by being proactive. First ask, What is my goal? And then build the habits to reach that goal. Do your habits reflect your goals?

I once heard a story about an overweight man who wanted to start running. To make running a habit, he decided to keep his gym shoes by his front door. Every day at 4:00 p.m., he went to the door and put on the shoes. For the first few months, he didn't leave his house. But every day, he put on his gym shoes. Putting on his gym shoes was the first habit he built.

After sixty days of putting on his shoes every day at 4:00 p.m., the man decided to go outside and take a walk. For the first week or so, he only walked to the end of his block; then, he ventured around the block. But every day at 4:00 p.m., he was outside, walking. Eventually, the walk got longer, and his weight started coming off. He started to run portions of the walk; over time, he ran more than he walked. Eventually, he only ran. Every day at 4:00 p.m., he put on his shoes and ran. Over time, his overall lifestyle became healthier, because he viewed himself as an athlete. He ate better—because that's what athletes do. He woke up earlier—because that's what athletes do. He got a gym membership—because that's what athletes do. And he started hanging out with other gym rats, talked fitness, drank protein shakes, ran Spartan races, played pickup basketball—because that's what athletes do.

If he would have judged himself at week one or two, when he was only putting his shoes on and not even leaving his home, he would still be overweight and unhealthy. If he listened to his roommate, who was eating pizza and chips on the couch, he would not be running Spartan races today. The point isn't that he needed to get up and run a marathon that first day. It's that to become the person you want to be, you can do it by building habits—doable habits—and making incremental progress. It is taking small steps every day toward a big vision.

If you are a couch potato, the first habit you want to build is not running a 5K every day. You'll fail miserably and go back to the couch. Instead, build a doable habit, like walking down the street to a certain spot every other day. Then build a new habit around the existing one.

Getting What You Deserve

For this habit-building to work, we need to change our relationship with ourselves. We do that by convincing ourselves that we deserve to meet our goals. We *deserve* good health. We *deserve* money in the bank. We *deserve* to be debt-free. We *deserve* an education. We *deserve* that dream job. We *deserve* that big house.

Many of us have been told exactly the opposite throughout our lives. The media feeds us images of beautiful people doing wonderful, fun things with a Coke in their hands, and we are led to believe our lives will magically look more beautiful, more wonderful and fun if we drink Coke. So we drink Coke and our lives don't magically change overnight. And we get upset because we're drinking Coke, wearing Levi's, eating McDonald's, driving a GMC, and using the latest iPhone, yet our lives are still messy. We are told we can earn the good life, but to get there we need to buy their product—and we do but still don't have the good life.

My self-esteem improved when it was not tied to something outside of me. It improved when it was not tied to my relationships. It improved when it was not tied to someone else's reaction to me. My self-esteem improved from inside of me rather than from how others reacted to me. Our self-esteem improves from within when we build more wins, do harder things.

It improves when we tell ourselves we deserve what we want and go out and take steps to make that desire a reality.

Did your parents tell you that you didn't deserve good things? If so, it's most likely because they were told the same. Like you, they are reacting to circumstances as they were conditioned to. But too often we disassociate from our dreams because our families tell us we don't deserve them when we absolutely do.

Think about when you wake up to get ready for work. I bet you do everything in the same order every day without thinking about it. Your subconscious hits the "get ready for work program" and you automatically do the things—in the same order—to get ready for work. It really is amazing, actually.

If you are a driver, think about when you learned how to drive. How you intentionally checked your mirrors, put on turn signals, thought about your route to get from point A to point B. Remember intentionally putting the car into Reverse or Park or Drive? And now? Do you even think about your route? Or do you often get in the car and disassociate and magically end up at your destination?

That disassociation is what we have been doing with our dreams for years. We disassociate from our dreams by sticking to our routine. We do what we've done because the people around us—usually our families—have done it that way.

I want us to be aware of our conditioning. Of our self-limiting beliefs. I want us to challenge that "I can't do that" refrain in our heads. Awareness is the first step to changing it. Once we become aware of our self-limiting beliefs, we can change them. We change our beliefs by realizing what we're doing, knowing that we deserve what we want; we change our beliefs by being intentional about changing our habits, with our goals—our North Star—firmly in focus. Every decision is made easier when we know what we're playing for. We commit to what we want and move toward it by taking small steps day after day.

Developing the Drive to Thrive

Back in 2013, I started my law firm, Thomas Law. Today, it is a thriving business, with myself and two excellent, hard-working attorneys, a director of operations who runs the show, and great people dedicated to helping our clients. But I want to let you in on a little truth: it wasn't always that way.

Immediately before opening Thomas Law, I worked at another firm. In that firm, I had an excellent opportunity to market myself, to let Chicago know that I was an excellent attorney representing injured people. It was a beautiful office—like something you'd see on television. *My* office was gorgeous. I was making pretty good money, I was learning how to market—my partner was an excellent marketer and I was there to learn how to take the next steps in my career.

But it didn't take. My personality, my being, wasn't a fit for that firm culturally. And I knew it. I could feel it. And I wanted to change it. I wanted to rebuild or recreate this firm into what I thought it *could* be, culturally.

But the person who owned and built the firm—and therefore earned the right to determine his firm's culture—had other ideas. It wasn't so much that he didn't want my cultural changes but more that the way it was running was working for him. The firm was his; he had built it from a single-employee (him) firm and he could do with it what he wanted.

Still, I fought to rebuild and reinvent his firm. Why? Because I was too scared to build my own. I was too afraid to build my own culture—to build a firm with my own personality. I was afraid to find people to work with who shared my vision.

Because I did not value myself.

I remember thinking, Who would want my firm to handle their personal injury case? Why would someone want to use Brian Thomas as opposed to the firm I was with? People were already using me to handle their cases, but I couldn't and didn't own my value outside of the firm. They didn't want me, I told myself; they wanted the firm and used me as a conduit to it.

All that turmoil was going on within me. The firm owner never said anything like that to me; he never made me feel less than. Never made me believe my thoughts were bad. Or that I was bad. That was all the hamster wheel in my head.

As my brain raced in angst, the firm's owner slowly started moving me out. My compensation package changed. Even though I could see the writing on the wall—that my time there was limited—I still had this fear that I wasn't *enough* to run a law firm on my own.

On my fortieth birthday, I got an email terminating our partnership agreement. I was with my buddy Gus, at the Big Ten tournament, watching the Fighting Illini play Indiana. I was stunned. I wanted to cry but had to pull myself together because I was in public "having a good time" on my fortieth birthday. I felt like more of a liability than a benefit to my family. And it punched me in the gut. Those punches started when I initially read that email and continued each time my brain went back to the thought that I was not wanted. That I was worthless. That I am a liability. That I suck. That I was *fired*.

But I couldn't spend all my time sulking because I had to figure out a way to open my own firm in sixty days. And I had to figure out how to do all of it on the fly: letterhead, business cards, telephone and fax numbers, telephone system, branding—my head was spinning from all the logistical hurdles.

The key here is that I had to convince myself to be the owner. The culture building was the easy part—it was the *I can do it*, or better stated, *CAN I DO IT?!* that was tough.

Every day was another day of convincing. I wish I could say that I took off and ran and *knew* I could do it. I *could* write that, but it would be a lie. The truth is that every day, getting up and getting to the office to do one more thing was an effort at convincing myself I could do it. The effort usually came during my commute into the office, when my brain would race with all the things that could go wrong. How my family would starve or how we would be forced into foreclosure. That is when the anxiety hit. It always hit at exactly the same place: at the merge between the Edens and Kennedy Expressways in Chicago.

It is really difficult to describe an anxiety attack. For me at least, my heart starts to race, I start to sweat, and I feel heavy with panic and doom. It feels like what I would expect a heart attack to feel like: pain across the chest into both arms, shortness of breath with an additional heavy blanket of dread covering me. The logical side of my brain tries to calm the anxious side, and it turns into a wrestling match tumbling through my head, overwhelming the circuits.

With my wife and doctor, I worked my way through the panic attacks and got on with my days. Rather than walking in every day convincing myself I could do it, I found that doing the work, day in and day out—with some days being easy and others not—convinced me that I *could* do the work.

I didn't have a choice but to get up and go in and do the work. I didn't have a choice but to hustle to get cases settled. I didn't have a choice but to go out there and find more work. The more work I did, the more I learned. It wasn't necessarily easy. It was like the weather: some days are beautiful and some days aren't. But getting up and showing up—*just showing up*—to put in another day of work taught me that what I wanted was within reach.

Being proactive was the cure. Doing the work was the cure. I wasn't anxious when I was working. My brain was focused on what I was doing. Every little thing I did, no matter how small, got me closer to what I was trying to accomplish. And every time I did those little things, my brain continued to hardwire them as habits. Mornings meant going to court. Then, at 4:00 p.m., I worked the phone, making callbacks and getting through my call list. Each time I did this, the anxiety melted away. Because I was focused—not on utter failure but on the judge in front of me or the person on the other end of the line.

And before long, I earned the goal of being able to manage my own law firm because I put habits in place that led to, you guessed it, being able to own and manage a law firm.

I couldn't measure myself against my former partner or other established firms. I had to measure myself against me last week. *Am I a little bit farther along than I was last week? What habits and rituals can I adjust for greater growth? What calculated investment can I make that will help me climb the mountain?*

That's when I made my first hire. At the time, Lucy Garcia was someone I had known for years. She worked as an assistant when I started at the firm that taught me trial work a decade before. Her story is amazing. She was born in a small town in Mexico; her family crossed the border and came to the United States when she was a teenager. She did not know how to speak English when her family settled in Chicago and pushed her into high school. And she fought. She fought to learn the language; she fought to learn the culture; she fought to earn money; she fought to find a place for herself. The reason why I love Lucy so much is because, like Rocky Balboa, she keeps fighting. That fighting spirit taught her to save every penny and now, less than twenty-five years later with a high school diploma, she owns her home and owns investment properties in Chicago and Mexico. She is a citizen of the United States. She epitomizes the American Dream. It's her example that makes it hard to believe that anyone with able body and mind can't also build wealth in the United States. She came here not knowing the language, not knowing the culture, with pennies to her name, and now she owns multiple properties and is an excellent example to her three girls. If anyone should be writing a book on how to build yourself into the person you want to be, it's Lucy Garcia.

So when she came to me and said she wanted to leave her firm and work for me, fear crept in. Did I have the revenue to support her? I was still earning less than in years past. How would I pay her? How could I afford her?

But I also clearly remember a voice inside saying, *You can't afford* not *having Lucy work with you.* And I remember talking with my wife, Amy, about it and we decided that I couldn't do this without Lucy. So we took the plunge, made the hire, and figured it out as we went.

Even then, I knew this was an excellent opportunity I had to figure out. And that's one thing I feel confident about: that while you are on your journey, while you are hard at work toward your North Star, you will be given opportunities to get you to your North Star. You will get there and you will have help.

So we jumped in together. Lucy had left her past

employer in part because they often didn't pay her. I promised I'd *never* allow that to happen. Though I paid less than her former employer, I made sure she got the money. The firm would not be where we are today without her hard work and investment.

Looking back, it really is amazing how far we've come as a firm. And we did that by showing up every day. We did that by trusting that things would work out as long as we showed up and did the work. Did we make mistakes? Absolutely. But we relied on the habit of showing up for ourselves, our clients, and the firm, and everything has worked out. And now we have bigger goals to attain—a bigger, grander picture that is to be made. And we'll keep showing up and doing the work, and that picture will fill itself in.

And that's the important thing about showing up. You show up and work gets done. You show up Tuesday and work gets done. Same thing on Wednesday, Thursday, and Friday. And the more you show up, the more works gets done. It starts to feed off itself. The more you show up, the more momentum is built.

Momentum is an awesome thing. The more you have, the easier the work becomes. In fact, it almost gets done on its own. Opportunities for more work start to appear. By conditioning yourself to say yes to new opportunities, you find more opportunities. When I was building my firm, I remember feeling like I was pushing a snowball uphill. It got too big for me to push it alone, so I hired Lucy to help. And we pushed. And the snowball got even bigger, so Lesley Hernandez started helping as well. Eventually, the hill started to flatten—and that snowball wasn't as hard to push. Then we started going downhill, and the snowball got bigger on its own.

But to get this momentum going, you first have to show up. If you don't show up, the magic doesn't happen. You can't just wait for things to happen. It doesn't work that way. You have to show up and do the work—to be proactive, to say yes, to get comfortable with being uncomfortable. By showing up and doing all these things, you will build momentum—and that momentum will get you to your North Star.

CHAPTER THIRTEEN

Invest in You

I WAS TRAVELING on the "L" back "home" to Oak Park. It was my first year of law school and I had my constitutional law book open in my lap. It was late and the train was empty.

Like the train, I was empty. I was lost. I was a whole lot of in between. Like the train, I was in between stops. But unlike the train, which was on the tracks, I felt directionless. I stared into the darkness of Chicago's West Side. I wasn't seeing what was there—I was seeing what was inside me, which existed outside the train: Fear. Darkness. An uncertain future.

A few months before, my father had moved out of the family home. After he left, I was also flung from the family home to go live with my father in his small studio apartment. It was completely foreign, because less than a year earlier I was high on life. A few months before, I was finishing up college in Champaign, Illinois. That I would graduate college was not in question. I was in the sun, drinking beer, flirting with college women (who were actually flirting back!), playing softball in the big park behind our house. It was a perfect few months. That's the way life was a few months earlier. It was my Goldilocks moment—everything was *perfect*.

Fast-forward a few months and I was lost in not only a Chicago winter but my own. The days of perfection within Champaign, Illinois, were gone. My parents' marriage wasn't the best, but I was away at school and couldn't see what it had become. Although their breakup wasn't surprising, it was still jarring, especially the way it was handled. We didn't talk about it. It just happened.

When I crossed that college graduation stage, I crossed from this full collegiate life to a frightening void punctuated by the constant I had—my parents' home, *my home*—being torn away from me and used as a bargaining chip. My life seemed to change in an instant.

I imagine this upheaval to be similar to living through a tornado. You hear the warning siren go off and you flee into the basement to get out of harm's way. You come upstairs ten minutes later and your physical life, all your possessions, are in tatters strewn across the remnants of your neighbor-hood. Your neighbors are all in the same position. What was a lawn is now debris. What was a street is now debris. What was home is now debris.

Imagine looking at that scene and being forced to sift through the wreckage of your life for weeks, months, or years and not acknowledging that a tornado came through to cause that wreckage.

That's the way we did things in my house growing up. My family did not acknowledge problems—we swept them under the rug and moved on. That's the way my parents' divorce was handled. My parents sent my girlfriend and me to Las Vegas as our graduation present. My father picked us up from the airport, dropped her off at her home, and then *dropped me off* at what had been our family home. That's how I was told he'd moved out. That's how I was told they were getting divorced. "Hope you had a great trip! See you later," he said as he pulled out of the driveway, leaving me there with what grew into more baggage than what I had taken to Las Vegas. There wasn't much discussion after that other than barbs being thrown back and forth as my parents jockeyed for their children's support.

As I started law school, my mother wanted the house to herself and I was banished to Oak Park to live with my father, and off to my father's studio apartment I went.

I had recently moved from a shitty fraternity house and soon found myself in a shittier tiny apartment in Oak Park, on Chicago's western border. Have you ever seen the 1950s television show *The Honeymooners*? The show takes place in Alice and Ralph Kramden's apartment in 1950s New York.

Michael Rougier/The LIFE Picture Collection/Shutterstock

Perhaps the owner of my father's apartment was a fan of the show because the kitchen from the Kramdens' apartment was a replica of the kitchen my father was forced to share with me between 1995 and 1997.

As I sat on that cold train, tired and alone, not looking forward to yet another night on the couch feet away from where my father slept, I felt fear. I felt overwhelmed. I was afraid and baffled. There was a realization that everything that was working wasn't working at all anymore. It had been so easy. I'd go to class—or not—and good grades came easily. We'd show up to the campus bars and it felt like kids would move out of the way so we could get a drink. A year before, everything had worked like magic, but one year later, the magic was gone and I was out in the cold, afraid, tired, and alone.

It was a jarring transition going from college to law school. Law school was not easy for me. And although I worked harder than I ever had in my life, decent grades were not coming easily. It was emotional not only having to do the work but then not having a place of my own—even a room of my own—to do the work in. I did not have a bed. I did not have a closet. I did not have a desk. I did not have the foundation I had come to take for granted.

Yet although I didn't know it then, the big picture remained. The big picture was being a lawyer and having an apartment and room to myself. I couch-surfed for a while—sleeping on friends' sofas in Chicago and my father's couch in Oak Park. I did this for two years. This is tough under any circumstance but is much tougher in law school. I found a job working as a clerk in a law firm and wore my father's oversized sports coats. I started making a little money. When my best friend returned home from London, we rented a place a block away from Wrigley Field. It was 1997 and I was twenty-four years old. I had a hand-me-down bed! I had my own room! I had a place to put my clothes! I was in my third year of law school, and although it still wasn't clicking, I was somewhat confident I'd graduate. The picture

I had formed on the cold train while I was alone and afraid started to come into focus. I was able to lay my head on my own pillow, in my own bed, with my clothes hanging in my closet—things I did not have my first two years of law school. That my checking account balance was cemented at $29.13 mattered but was less important considering I could close the door to my small room, have a space for my clothes, and be able to sleep soundly in my own space.

On those cold train trips back to Oak Park, a picture had formed in my head. A picture of what I wanted. Two years later, I was living in that picture.

What Picture Is in Your Head?

I mentioned earlier how Manny Khoshbin, the real estate tycoon, drew a picture of what his life would be like one day. He included the large house with palm trees, a beautiful wife, and several high-end luxury sports cars. Twenty years later, he was living that life.

To go from being a sixteen-year-old K-Mart store clerk to a multimillionaire real estate tycoon took a lot of work. Manny didn't just draw a picture, sit back on the couch, and wait for the big home, beautiful wife, and millions of dollars. There was a lot of work that took him from point A to point T.

Since drawing the picture of my life at twenty-three,

I have drawn several other pictures. Pictures that included children, a nice suburban home in an excellent school district, nice cars, and some level of financial comfort. That picture had me as the managing partner of a law firm. All these things I drew in the past came to fruition. Like Manny Khoshbin, I did not draw the picture and wait. I worked. I worked hard. I learned the law, and opportunities came. Most of the time, the opportunities came disguised as setback or failure. For example, I was fired from my second job as a lawyer. It was at a firm where I felt sick to my stomach every time I entered the building. I hated going to that job. I wanted to find another job in another area of law. I wanted to build toward the picture I had in my head at the time, which was greater financial independence, building a family, and one day getting the suburban home with the nice yard. Then I lost that job. I lost the job I thought I needed to get the nice house in the suburbs.

I could not have been more wrong. The universe conspired with me without my knowledge. Since I wasn't going to quit, the universe (or God or Source) took that job away from me. Losing that job ultimately put me on the path to financial comfort I have now. I lost that job, which led me to another job working for a plaintiff's personal injury firm. At that firm, I learned how to manage a caseload, talk to and manage clients, go to court, and handle arbitrations and mediations and trial. Seven years later another opportunity came my way and I made a very difficult decision to leave that firm and move my clients to another. The new firm was the next step in my education in being a law firm owner. As I shared before, after a few years at that firm, although happy with the money I was making, I was not happy with the culture. The universe gave me another push—disguised as a negative—and I started my own practice. And with a lot of hard work, that practice helped build the picture I drew in my head and now live.

Each picture I have dreamed up has come true.

So pay attention to the pictures you dream up.

How would your life look if you knew you could not fail? Take some time and think about that. As you do it, listen to any limiting thoughts that come in, smile at the thought, and dismiss it. The goal isn't to listen to the thought but to acknowledge it, smile that you see that niggling thought there, and then let it go like a wisp of smoke.

What life do you see behind the smoke of your negative thoughts? What is behind all that smoke—the smoke that is "I can't because I'm too _____?" Behind the smoke is the picture you can work toward. That's the goal. Tell yourself about the house you visualize. Tell yourself about where the house is located. Is it in the mountains? On the beach? In a high-rise? Who are the people around you in that picture?

Are you married? How many children—if any—do you have? What do you do for fun? What do you do for a living? How do you maintain that lifestyle?

Act as If

Act as if. Act as if you are already in that picture. Once you start acting as if you are in that picture, your subconscious will start to move you toward that picture. Opportunities will come that would not have otherwise—or that you would not have seen as an opportunity. Act as if.

As you start to act as if, also do a self-inventory. Like the smoke that dissipated as you pictured your dream, your mental backpack will weigh you down as you move toward that picture. You need to be aware of that baggage—very likely a product of your environment—so that when the backpack gets heavy, you recognize what is weighing it down and let it go.

Although much of this baggage comes from your family, friends, and environment, do not judge them. Most people are creating systems and beliefs that help them though this world; you pick up those systems and beliefs by your proximity. The goal isn't to shame a loved one for their belief. The goal is to recognize a belief that will not get you to that picture you drew. If that system or belief doesn't get you to that picture, let it go. That's why awareness is so important. If you aren't aware of the belief, how are you going to let it go? That's why the subconscious phrase, "I can't because I'm too _____" is so important because now you recognize that belief when it comes to you. And you push past it.

That big goal of yours, that big picture, will cause you to have to reframe some of your beliefs.

Attitude toward Work

Examine your attitudes toward employment. Do you have a job when you really want a career? If your big goals require something other than a job, then you can reframe employment. Can you reframe employment from a job to a career? Does your employment provide you an opportunity to advance? What does advancement look like in that job? Is that a job you want to advance in?

My first job was at McDonald's on Butterfield Road, in Elmhurst. I loved working there. I worked with plenty of high school part-timers, along with immigrants who worked harder than anyone I had ever seen—working eight hours at the McDonald's I worked at, and then driving to another McDonald's and working another eight-hour shift.

Although I loved working there, it wasn't the career I wanted. I could have made it one—I could have learned how to get into management and then figure out how to invest in my own franchise and expand that business, but it wasn't what I wanted. There was potential for advancement, and potentially that advancement would get me to the picture I dreamed up—it just wasn't the advancement I wanted. It wasn't the advancement that stirred my soul. That made McDonald's a job for me.

Reframe your employment. Is what you're doing a job or career? What is the end goal? Does your employment advance you to that goal? If not, find different employment. Also recognize that just because your job can get you to your end goal doesn't mean that your current employment will get you there. If you want to be a general manager at a McDonald's, yet the GM at the McDonald's where you work keeps you in drive-thru and you have little opportunity to move up the ladder, then you have to move to a different McDonald's. In a similar way, my employment at just any firm as a lawyer was not the position or experience I needed to get me where I wanted to go.

Reframing your employment from being just a job that pays your bills and gets you to the weekend so you can blow off steam to being an investment in your future is a game changer in terms of getting you closer to that bigger picture. If working drive-thru at McDonald's gets you closer to the goal of owning that McDonald's, learning and mastering your position is an investment rather than simply having to be there. What's the next thing you have to master after drive-thru? Grill? Front counter? Talk to the manager to get experience in those other areas to get you closer to your goals.

Building a Family Foundation

Another area we can reframe is family. Reframe from "having kids" or having a baby daddy to building a family. Anyone can have a kid. It takes much more work to build a family.

Each privilege described in the privilege race is related to building a family unit. Those privileges are:

- Parents are still married to each other

- Father figure in the home

- Access to private education

- Access to a free tutor

- Never had to worry about their cell phone being shut off

- Don't have to help Mom or Dad pay household bills

- Don't have to pay for college (outside of athletic scholarship)

- Never had to wonder about their next meal

The first two are directly related. The next six are indirectly related to having an intact family in that it is so much easier to build wealth when two people do it together. According to the United States Census Bureau, one in four children live without a father figure in the home.[26] In those homes, kids are four times more likely to live in poverty, seven times more likely to become pregnant as a teen, more likely to abuse drugs and alcohol, twice as likely to drop out of high school, and are at greater risk of committing crime and going to prison.[27]

If this data is true, it points to the importance of having a father figure in the home with children.

It is also much easier to build wealth with two people creating a foundation, without children, rather than having to build the foundation while caring for children. Think of it like this: If you are building a home from the ground up, how much easier would it be to build that home while you don't live in it? When building a foundation for our family, it will be easier to build a financial and career foundation without children as part of the build.

To build that foundation, invest in yourself. Invest in an education to get the job you want versus having a job in order to pay for formula. Invest in a career in an area you want. Learn how to save money. Learn how to invest money. Learn how to manage your money so it works for you in the future.

Find a partner. Find a partner you can build with. Invest in a person who shares your goals and dreams, and it will be easier to build on the foundation you have. Perhaps your partner also has a foundation; they also have savings and a picture of how they want life to look in ten years.

I was thirty-five years old when our first child was born. My wife and I earned well over six figures in income. We had savings. We owned our home. We had the ability to save. After Sammy was born, our expenses skyrocketed. We had to pay for diapers, formula, a breast pump, a crib, clothes, bottles, toys, more clothes, more diapers, more formula, more food, pediatrician visits. We both worked, so childcare was a huge expense. Our ability to save ended soon after Sam's birth, and most months, we had to dip into our savings to make ends meet. The financial cost of having a child shocked our system even though we were in a great financial position when we had him.

There's also the huge emotional cost. Not sleeping. Juggling work obligations with trying to be a good father or mother. Not having "me time" anymore. We were not able to travel on a whim. We were less able to walk down the street and get dinner out without packing up that big diaper bag, the stroller, and car seat. It took twenty minutes just to get out of the house versus what we were used to: throwing on clothes, hailing a cab, and going to dinner.

Everything changed. And it wasn't all bad, obviously. Much of it was awesome. I got to see my son smile at me when I walked into a room. I got to hang out with him, play catch, or have lemonade on the porch with him in his little chair after work.

But it would have been much more difficult to manage the emotional and financial hardship of having a child had I done that at twenty-two years old. Amy and I intentionally got all our ducks in a row before we had a child and it was still tough. How would I have done that while I was in college?

The decision to have a child when I had sufficient income and resources was difficult. Remember: if you choose to have children at a young age and then have difficulty making ends meet, it's not because of systemic racism but because you made a choice to have children before your finances were in order.

The decision to have children when you have insufficient resources increases the likelihood that your child will have insufficient resources. That decision makes it much more likely that your children will remain at the starting line of the privilege race. It is not only racism that keeps our children at the starting line; our decisions do too.

Let's be clear: being a college graduate does not make a man a good father. You don't need to graduate college and have a good-paying job to be an excellent father. Being a great father is more about being present in your child's life than it is about what you can give them.

But why not do both? Why not be able to provide your child a home in a nice neighborhood with great schools?

The self-investment of education directly relates to building a family. You are building the foundation to be able to provide for your family. Building a career provides your future self a foundation so that when you have that child, you are able to move into a kid-friendly home, neighborhood, and school district.

Being in a committed relationship also provides a foundation for the family. You can build that foundation together. And after that foundation is laid by finding jobs within careers, finding opportunities within the career, saving, and buying a home, you can then build on it. You will see brokerage accounts with investment gains; you'll see your home's value increase; you may buy that dream house in the neighborhood you want to be in. You will see your kids go to good schools and have opportunities to do things you did not.

This advice may seem a bit old-fashioned. I get it. But having lived this life and seeing the recipe of families around me both as a child and an adult, *this is how it is done.*

This photograph was taken in September 2013 after we purchased our home. We were still having work done on the home, but we would come in nightly and eat dinner on picnic blankets on the dining room floor. My kids are four and one here, playing in the backyard after one of those dinners. Getting them to leave the yard after this photograph was taken involved a lot of tears.

This photograph is so important to me because of the

decades of hard work before that got me to this moment in time. The toiling in law school. The waiting tables in law school along with clerking to make ends meet. The grind from each job that gave us the opportunity to put together just enough money to stretch to get to this moment. The betting on ourselves to get here. The sacrifice it took both before *and after* the photo was taken. The waking up at 3:24 a.m. wondering how I was going to earn enough to pay the mortgage. But then I look at this photograph and I think of my kids having this home with this yard in an excellent school district, and I know that everything it took for us to get there was worth it.

Thriving is so much easier when you build on a foundation with a partner sharing your vision.

Surviving alone is not enough.

Surviving is going to a job with no prospects for advancement because you need to get diapers.

Surviving is turning government aid into a lifestyle.

Surviving is going through life earning less than you deserve while getting hits of dopamine through sex, entertainment, alcohol, or drugs.

You survive—but what do you accomplish? You survive—but do you *thrive*? Did you ever really *go for it*? Or do you simply punch in and punch out every day of your life?

You Can't Be What You Don't See

We recreate the lives of the people we see around us. We do that because we do not know alternatives. We understand that there are alternatives, but we do not see and know those alternatives. We know France exists, but can we appreciate France if we have never studied it? Can we appreciate France if we've never been there? Can we learn to be French if we're not surrounded by the French people and culture?

One hundred years ago, life was much more limited. If we wanted to learn French, we had to find a group of French people or go to France to do it. Today, we can learn French from the comfort of our homes. The internet brings France to us.

The same is true with the type of success you crave. Billionaire podcaster Ed Mylett has said that success leaves clues. You can find people you want to be like and listen to their lessons. Do you want to be like Apple founder Steve Jobs? Read his book. Do you love Will Smith and want to imitate him? Watch his interviews and learn about him. How did he do what he did? What is his mindset? What challenges did he face along the way? How did he get through those challenges? What's the first thing he does in the morning? Does he have a gratitude ritual? Does he meditate? What can you incorporate into your life today that will have an effect tomorrow?

I've seen YouTube videos where a person shows us an elegant mansion, walks to the front door, and says to the person who opens the door: "You have a beautiful house, what do you do?"

Of course, getting in your car and driving to a neighborhood with manicured lawns, ringing doorbells, and asking people what they do for a living could have you answering questions in the back of a police car. Yet people like Manny Khoshbin have written books. You can invest in those books for less than twenty dollars on Amazon. If you don't have money for that, then go to a podcasting platform and find an interview with these people. Listen to what they have to say and find out if you want to invest the money to learn even more from their books.

Maybe real estate is not your thing. What is? Find someone successful in an area that interests you and go out and learn how that person became a success. It is so easy to do today. You can have a mentor who doesn't even know you exist. I think about lessons I've learned from Ed Mylett, Lewis Howes, Lisa Nichols, and others daily, and none of them know I exist. Still, they are my mentors. They—and hundreds of others—have thousands of hours of content on the internet on how to level up.

That's why you invested in this book.

Seek out mentors—people you know and people you

don't—and learn how you can get to where they are. You can't be what you don't see. Thankfully, because of technology, you can see anything you want and learn to be it.

The first step is consciously deciding you want it.

CHAPTER FOURTEEN

Live for More Than the Weekend

IN MY TWENTIES, I lived in Chicago, Illinois. It was a three-bedroom, one-bathroom apartment one block away from Wrigley Field. Back then, weekends consisted of people coming over for beers and shooting pool, and going to The Red Lion, a neighborhood haunt (literally, it is haunted) in Lincoln Park. Saturdays would begin the way Friday night ended: beer in hand awaking to the possibilities of another day in paradise. We would sometimes shower but would always head over to Wrigley Field. We were there so often that we made friends with an usher who saved us seats—right field, fourth-row seats on the aisle—if we arrived early enough. Having four seats in the fourth row on the aisle behind Sammy Sosa was like having a golden ticket back in 1998.

We'd drink beer in the glorious sun, remind the bums out in left field that they suck, jeer the opponent's right fielder (Larry Walker was the best; we'd chant his name and he'd take a lighter out of his back pocket, light it overhead, and sway his arm with our chant), and root on our Cubs. Wrigley Field is a church, and we were among its parishioners.

Every weekend was celebrated. Our parties were so epic, friends of friends asked us to host bachelor parties. They'd sit rooftop at a Cubs game and we'd throw the party in our apartment afterward. D-List celebrities wandered in to hang out. We were friendly with the beat cops, who'd tell us to keep it down with a wink. A card game was going all the time. The parties were, well, heavily attended. To get from the front of the apartment to the back, it was easier to leave, walk through the gangway, and reenter through the back door to get to the beer and booze in the kitchen. It was the love of our youth and summer sun in Chicago. We celebrated well.

If you told me back then to live for more than the weekend, I would have promptly laughed in your face. We were having too much fun on the weekend.

And life should be good and fun. Life should be enjoyed and lived. I was right to enjoy it then.

Live like That Today

Our society expects us to work hard for forty or fifty years and retire and enjoy our Golden Years. My grandfather-in-law, Bernie Meyers, dispelled that myth years ago. Yes, my in-laws wintered in Florida and I thought that was the pinnacle, yet I remember him saying that every time the phone rang, they worried about which of their friends had died. You know when the phone rings at 3:00 in the morning? That's the way they felt every time the phone rang.

His message was clear: don't wait until you're seventy to live. Do it today.

We can all get behind the why—but how?

Why do Friday and Saturday feel so different to us from Monday? Why do we do the things we love most on weekends rather than weekdays? Is it that we're escaping our Monday through Friday lives? If so, can we learn to enjoy the work-week such that Saturday is no longer an escape from the grind but an extension of the fun?

Impact of the Growth Mindset

Mindset is the key. I understand needing a Friday night out, having a bit too much to drink, and dancing like nobody's watching. I get the escape from the everyday grind. We need those days too. Yet if we change our Monday through Friday mindset from "must work to pay bills" to "investment in myself to move toward a goal," can we escape the dreariness of a nine-to-five?

That barbeque you hosted on Saturday afternoon is an

investment in your friends and family. That Friday night out is rest and relaxation. That day spent lying on the beach or beside the pool with a book is an investment in your mental health.

Monday morning's arrival in the office is an investment in *you*. Getting up, putting on work clothes, is an investment in your future self. The money you earn can be invested for a home or stocks or education or vacation.

There is no need to escape the daily grind when it's no longer a grind, but growth. What I did in my twenties was use the money I earned from my Monday through Friday life to escape that Monday through Friday life.

Yet if our Monday through Friday lives clearly impact our future selves rather than just providing a means of support to get to our weekends, there is no need to escape the daily grind—because it's not a grind when it's an investment in our growth.

Not living solely for the weekend means making investments in ourselves. Here's the thing about investing: it is not fun . . . especially at first. Which is more fun today? Taking a hundred dollars and investing it in stock or taking it and buying something you want? I enjoy investing, yet I can tell you I'd much rather take that money and go buy something with it. It is so much more fun to get that immediate dopamine hit than putting a hundred dollars into stock.

But what is going to put future you in a better position? That money in Pfizer stock or that money spent at the bar? Having spent plenty of money both on stocks and at the bar, looking back on it all, I regret not buying more stock. Pfizer stock is an asset; going to the club is a liability. Invest in assets—purchase liabilities after your make that investment.

Some of that bar experience was well worth it—I met fun people, laughed, had a bunch of fun. I did things we still laugh about twenty-five years later. The message is *not* don't enjoy life.

You can have fun and invest in yourself too.

Investing in yourself means education. Investing in education may mean forgoing making money while you invest in yourself. Think about that investment of money into Apple stock; money invested today could be used on something more fun than Apple stock. But hopefully in the future that investment will reap rewards. Like stock, after the investment in education is made, you'll earn more.

Education can mean a lot of different things today. I believe it means getting your high school diploma. That is the floor to be earned. From there, invest in what you want to do. If you want to go into a trade, invest in trade school; invest in an apprenticeship and invest in educating yourself about that trade and how to earn the money you want to earn—and deserve to earn—from that trade. Does that mean owning your own business? If it does, then learn how to do it from others who have done the work.

There are so many different routes to financial and professional "success" than the one I took. One reason for that is everyone defines "success" differently. How I define success is different from how you define it. The way you define success may be different from your mother's definition.

But there is one constant: self-investment. Showing up for the future you. Having grit. Grit is the sustained passion and perseverance for long-term goals. In her best-selling book *Grit: The Power of Passion and Perseverance*, psychologist Angela Duckworth said people with grit maintain effort and interest over years despite setbacks, adversities, plateaus, and successes. They follow through, have the fortitude, and possess the courage to stay the course.[28]

We might look at successful people and think they woke up that way. We don't see all the hard work they put in day in and day out. One example is Kobe Bryant. Kobe worked *harder* than everyone else. Just one example of this was in the 2012 Olympic Games. One morning Kobe called a trainer named Rob at 4:15 a.m. and asked if he was available to go to the gym and work on conditioning. Rob got to the gym before 5:00 a.m. and Kobe was already working out drenched in sweat. They worked out for two hours—both on the court and with weights. Exhausted, Rob left to take a nap before the 11:00 a.m. practice. Rob later returned before practice as Kobe's teammates, such as LeBron James and Kevin Durant, were arriving. Rob saw Kobe shooting jump shots and went over to him to compliment him on the morning workout. He asked Kobe what time he left. Kobe looked at him and said that he decided to stay until he made eight hundred shots—which he'd just finished. He had practiced from 4:30 a.m. until the 11:00 a.m. scheduled practice with the other Olympians. This was Kobe in 2012. A man who already had five NBA Championships and an Olympic gold medal (soon to be two); he was still waking up and working out for seven hours *before* practice.

You don't have to get to work seven hours before everyone else. You do have to invest in yourself and *do the work*. Successful people continue showing up and doing the work. Day after day after day. Successful people do the extra work necessary to reach their goals rather than only what is expected.

When we move toward our life goals—our North Star—it makes it easier to get that extra work done. It's easier because the work isn't only for a certain company, it's for you. That overtime you're working isn't only for your boss, it goes toward your investment in your trip to France, or your down payment on your dream home, or so you can start your own business. You're working hard because you're moving toward your best you.

Someone once said that there are two types of people in the world, the bumblers and the pointers. The bumblers get up and try to do something, fail, and get up the next day and try again. The pointers laugh about the failures of the bumbler and never try themselves. The great thing about bumbling and failing is that you learn. Being on that path, while bumbling, will move you forward. However, the pointer sits stagnant. Guess who ends up moving forward? Meanwhile, there is no benefit at all in pointing.

People will have opinions on what you're doing. The question is whether *you* are happy with what you're doing and where you are. If you listen to the pointers, will you continue saving and working and striving toward that goal of buying a house for your family? Or will you stay next door to the person telling you it's impossible?

The World Doesn't Erect Statues of Critics

Your investment journey will be challenging. But remember that you're out there trying while people who *aren't* trying knock you to make themselves feel better. Remember that you're not here to one-up them but to one-up yesterday's version of you.

The great thing about self-investment is the momentum.

You'll not only reach goals but surpass them. You'll vacation on South Beach and you are still investing in the next version of yourself. Is that an investment toward an African safari? Is that investment a new home for your family? A new car? A healthier body? A healthier mindset? Whatever that goal is for you—you have learned how investing in yourself manifests rewards. You are not afraid of a little work. You've done it and saw how it brought rewards.

My parents gave me an excellent opportunity. But that opportunity doesn't mean anything if I didn't work at it. My great fortune was my parents modeled hard work for me. I saw that hard work translated into a more comfortable living. We went from having AT&T's trash as furniture to a very comfortable lifestyle. I equated that socioeconomic advance-ment with their grit, the fact they showed up day after day after day. They showed up despite difficulties. They showed up despite racism. They showed up despite my father getting harassed by his white coworkers in the 1980s.

That's how we do. Despite the adversity—despite the kidney transplants, despite the failing hips, despite the pulmonary embolism, despite the tax debt, despite the unpaid mortgage, despite family stress, despite some mistakes and poor decision-making—I kept showing up. Some days showing up meant getting up at 5:00 a.m. and working thirteen-hour days. Some days meant getting to the office and just getting *one thing* done.

I promise self-investment will put you closer to where you want to be ten years from now. While the pointer who was criticizing you is still struggling to scrape together rent, you have money coming in and are living comfortably in your home. Is it still a struggle at times? Of course. But your struggles are next-level because your baseline is higher. You're struggling to top $100,000 in income rather than just struggling. You're struggling to have $1,000,000 in investments rather than just struggling.

You are thriving rather than just surviving.

Investing is boring, until you see the rewards. Putting fifty dollars into the stock market is boring. But continually making that investment over time will grow into hundreds of thousands of dollars. That's fun! I've invested in the stock market for over twenty years. It was forced on me when I was enrolled in a 401k plan. Twenty years ago, seeing that I had $2,300 in an account didn't excite me. But I knew on some level that it was the right thing to do and that I would one day benefit from it.

Knowing which voice to listen to is a part of maturity. I've listened to both voices. I've spent 401k money on beer, clubs, and feeble attempts to make me look cool. I've also listened to the other voice that says, "One day this will work out—just keep going." And then when I get there—in year three of law school, or after the bar exam results are posted, or when a transplanted kidney starts working in my body—I see that all the work and stress and sacrifice was worth it.

Nowadays I have a number of goals in front of me every day, and I feel more fulfilled than I ever did back when I was drinking the day away at Wrigley Field. I own my life. The investments I've made in my life give me ownership over it, and I'm proud of that.

It's okay if you're not there today. (Frankly, if I'd picked up this book when I was living for the weekend twenty years ago, I would have used it as a coaster.) You are where you are today—and you're supposed to be there—but do not stay there forever.

Know that one day, the shenanigans will start feeling empty. You'll be in a different club, but the scene will be the same. The days and nights will run together. It will turn into the same party night after night after night. When that happens—and I promise it will—remember this book you're using as a coaster and pick it up and start reading. Maybe it will speak to you. And maybe, just maybe, you'll start thinking about how you can build the life you want versus using the weekend to escape the life you have.

CHAPTER FIFTEEN

Why Be Reasonable?

IT WAS THE SUMMER of 2021. My business was humming along. I'd been very fortunate and the work had led to opportunities to grow the business even more.

Yet I lived with hesitation. That hesitation had been there a while. It was an inaudible whisper that was more like a feeling. That feeling was my brain saying, Am I doing what I am passionate about? Or am I doing what I have been programmed to do?

William Cloud was my high school English teacher. He was the kind of teacher where I knew I was being impacted by him as I sat in his room. He didn't only teach me about writing. He taught me to enjoy the process of writing; he cheered me on and told me how much he enjoyed my work. He encouraged us to look at the world from a different perspective and learn about that perspective by writing about it. I am grateful for Mr. Cloud because his influence is one I carry with me today.[29]

Mr. Cloud gave me a passion to write. Yet, not terribly long ago, I was in the routine of being an attorney. My days were very busy—but I missed doing that thing I was passionate about: writing.

I had not been writing. I had become so busy with work that I lost my enjoyment of putting words on a page and sculpting those words into a message. Rather than continuing to ignore that nagging feeling, I started to get up one hour earlier in the morning to write. Using Jerry Seinfeld's method to writing jokes, I used a monthly dry erase calendar and marked off each day I wrote. The interesting thing was that as I continued writing and marking off days, I didn't want to break the streak, and that is why I wrote—not to break that streak! That streak developed into a habit of writing most mornings. Writing again awoke my dream to write a book. As I wrote, I asked myself the question, How does one write a book? That question caused me to seek out people who have written books, who put me in touch with people and resources that helped turn words on a page into a book. It was listening to that whisper or feeling that pushed me out of the lawyer lane for a couple of hours each week and put me back into my dream of *writer*.

Another dream I have is to buy a Porsche 911. I struggle to write that because it sounds obnoxious. But it's a nice car, and I have that dream, and I have been incredibly close to buying something totally impractical for someone with payroll to make and a mortgage to pay. Didn't I just get myself out of a financial pickle?

Still, that car sits gleaming in my mind's eye. Me in the driver's seat, that Porsche shield on the steering wheel staring at me as I listen to the purr of the engine. Seeing the valet open the door for my wife as she gets out of the car at a restaurant. Taking it to the detail place to get it washed.

How can I know if it was worth it unless I do it? I may regret it in the Chicago winter when it sits unused for five months; will I think about money that could have been put to work in other places? Or will I think about the next time I can hear the rumble of the engine and feel the power pushing me on the Edens Expressway?

The only way I will know is to do it.

My friend Robin recently had a reading with a medium. She told me how the medium was able to connect with her recently deceased father, and he told her, "Do it now."

That message resonated with me. Look, I'm a kidney transplant patient. I've had my kidney for sixteen years. The transplant I had when I was thirteen years old lasted nineteen years.

I try not to think about the transplant much. I don't walk around considering myself a "kidney transplant patient." But there are certainly ways my life is different from yours because of the transplant: I take medication twice daily and have for decades, my hips are bone on bone with arthritis, making it difficult to walk from time to time; the coronavirus pandemic was difficult on my family because the medication I'm on suppresses my immune system, making me more susceptible to viruses, even after being vaccinated.

That said, I pop my medication in and start my day and do the things I would do if I wasn't a transplant patient. Then, when it's time to wind down, I pop my medication and brush my teeth and go to bed.

The kidney transplant gives me some context. The good health I am in can be taken away from me in a moment. This kidney can fail and I could be seeking a donor while on dialysis. Or even without dialysis, I could see the quality of my life significantly decrease because of the decreased kidney function. I've seen it happen twice before. It can happen again.

That's why "do it now" has some significance. If not now, when? When it's safe? When will it be safe to live your dream? When you have X amount saved in the bank? Maybe, but at the same time, why? What is that dream? Do you really need X amount in the bank to go live a great life? Why do you need X amount in the bank to go live a great life? Is that an arbitrary number? Or did you create that rule to limit what you can do?

I listened to the whisper and invested an hour a day to write. I didn't need X amount saved in the bank. I needed to be more efficient with my time. We're all busy, but I bet you can shave an hour off social media and television time to devote to that thing you used to love.

Can you do what you want to do now?

If so, go do it. *Do it now.*

Just like my life has the context of two kidney transplants and chronic kidney disease, your life has context too. *Do it now.*

And if you can't do it now, then put a plan into place so that it will get done. That may mean getting that massage once a month because you can't afford once a week. But you are moving toward the life you want. Be intentional about living the life you want to live.

*   *   *

Let's consider for a moment what's reasonable. If you gain something without a great amount of effort, are you thrilled by it when you get it? Why set the bar at "reasonable"? There's no work involved. It's reasonable that you should be able to get a job, bring home a paycheck, and pay your bills. You can be grateful when that gets done, but are you *thrilled*? Are you enthusiastic to be surviving?

I'm completely grateful for being able to get up, put my feet on the floor, and walk to my bathroom; I'm grateful for living today. I am grateful for my good health. But I'm not *enthusiastic* about walking downstairs to make a pot of coffee. It's reasonable that would get done. I'm totally grateful for

247

my warm bed, my family's home, and food in the refrigerator, but I'm not floored by it. Although I'm fortunate to have these necessities, it's reasonable that I should have them. Just like it's reasonable you should have them too.

Reasonable for me is getting my family on a plane and traveling to California and staying in some nice resort and lying poolside for a week. We've done it several times and I love each time we do it, so purchasing airfare and reserving rooms at a resort is not that big of a deal.

A few months ago, a neighbor told us about their planned trip next summer to Greece. Another set of neighbors is planning that trip too. My wife looked at me in those moments and said, "We're going to Greece next summer." And honestly, why not? I don't like flying and I don't speak Greek, but I would love to see Athens and Santorini. Both would be amazing for my children. And we'd get to experience it with some friends.

Taking a daddy / daughter trip to Paris is unreasonable. She is in love with Paris because of an "Around the World" project she did years ago in preschool. Getting on a plane, just my daughter and me for five days in Paris would be a little unreasonable because—rightfully so—my wife and son would hate not being invited to Paris. But if we make traveling more routine, a part of who we are, we can make the unreasonable—a quick daddy/daughter trip to Paris—a little more reasonable.

(Since initially writing those words, my family went to Paris—some evidence that what you put your mind to can come to fruition.)

We get one life and it is meant to be enjoyed. We are meant to have fun. We are meant to laugh. We are meant to love. We have the opportunity to live a great adventure—will we take it? Or will we get jobs, bring home a paycheck, get our bills paid, and watch Netflix? Sure, we can be grateful for that life—but can't we do that *and more*? Can we do that reasonable stuff and live the life of our dreams? The big question is whether you are able to say a hearty yes to your adventure.[30]

Is being reasonable adventurous? Is packing up your car and driving west—without a destination—a bit more of an adventure? Where do you want to be? Are you called to go to Jerusalem? Then ask yourself what you are doing to get there. You may live in Atlanta and get in your car and drive a few hours to get to the Florida coast—and I'm sure it's perfectly fun and enjoyable. But does being on Longboat Key for the seventeenth time make your soul soar? Or did that happen when you saw the sun rise over Mount Haleakala on Maui? Continue to enjoy Longboat Key, Florida, but get your ass to Maui too!

Does your heart soar when you sing? Does your heart soar when you create? Does your heart soar when you fly? Then do more of that! Figure out a way to get more of the stuff you love to do and that fills you up rather than what you do to pay bills.

Living Intentionally

After being a lawyer for over twenty years, being an author was a little unreasonable for me. Yet writing speaks to me, so I intentionally created time to write. In so doing, I created the space to write a book.

If you want to enjoy a Cubs game in July, telling your boss you are taking a day off to go to a Cubs game is living intentionally. Deciding you want to learn to sing and finding a voice coach to teach you is living intentionally. Deciding you want to go to Paris and opening up a "Paris Savings Account" to save money for the trip is living intentionally. Dream big and then go after it.

Is your dream to own your own business? Great. Make it happen. What do you need to do to make your business a reality? Millions of people have owned their own businesses—seek a few out and ask for their help. There are so many resources to get business help, like the Small Business Association and Urban League.

But you need to be intentional about it. You need to say, "I want X" and then sit down and plan out the steps you need to take to get there. And then very intentionally *do the work.*

In his book *Powershift,* Daymond John interviewed Lindsey Vonn. Lindsey Vonn knew as a child that she wanted to ski in the Olympics. She was so certain in this knowledge that when she was nine years old, she decided the 2002 Salt Lake City Olympics would be her first appearance at the Games. Lindsey and her father mapped out a ten-year plan that would get her to those Games, which included events she would have to win and money she would have to raise. She broke down this ten-year goal with dozens of mini goals that would get her to where she wanted to be. As she knocked out goal after goal, she inched her way closer and closer to the 2002 Games and eventually succeeded, made the team, and earned a silver medal in her first Olympics.

She was very intentional about not only her big goal but also the mini-goals she would have to knock out to get herself there.

Just like Lindsey Vonn had an unreasonable goal, you do too. And just like she did, you too can break down your goal into bite-size pieces. What is the best way to eat an elephant? One bite at a time.

Lewis Howes told a story about working hard on his goal of making the Olympics with the United States handball team.[31] He talked about the bite-size pieces he broke up his goal into. Ultimately, he did not reach that goal. But his takeaway was everything he experienced while trying to reach it: playing handball around the world with "USA" across his chest, hearing the national anthem when participating in international games, traveling the world, getting to play handball with the best players in the world. Even though he didn't reach the goal, his experiences while trying to reach the goal were the reward.

What do you want to do? Build your plan to do it. The new thing you do to get you closer to your goal becomes easier as you do it. To put these words on the page, I built the habit of writing daily. After building that habit, I enlisted other people to show me what other habits I needed to build a book. As I learned those other habits, the habit of writing became second nature.

Thirteen years ago, when Amy became pregnant with our firstborn, we lived in a two-bedroom condo. We had to walk up to the third floor to get to our unit. That was fine for two people but much more difficult for two people plus a stroller, car seat, diaper bags, and a baby. We set out to buy a new home and paid more than I thought we would ever be able to afford. When I think about the jump we made to get into that home, what was so financially frightening at the time is now routine.

We build on our successes. What was a pain point five years ago, after doing it for days and weeks and months, eventually becomes routine.

Your education is a great example. When you were in sixth grade, the concepts you saw were difficult for you. Maybe a specific type of math was difficult. But after a year of doing that work and then doing work beyond that in seventh and eighth grade, concepts you learned in sixth grade were easy. By building on a foundation, the work you do today will get you to the next level in your life.

The same is true at the gym. A person may start by lifting eighty-five pounds on the bench press. They continue at that weight for a while, but the more they do it, the stronger they get. Soon, eighty-five pounds becomes ninety-five pounds. It continues to increase as the person continues to work out, continues showing up, and what was once difficult becomes easy. The concept of lifting eighty-five pounds is almost laughable, although at some time in the past, it was difficult to do.

The key is to keep showing up. To keep doing the work.

Get Uncomfortable

I believe our brains are designed to keep us safe by seeking to keep us comfortable. The problem with comfort is that you don't learn anything there.

If I want to learn how to play golf, I have to get uncomfortable, risk my ego being significantly bruised, and swing a golf club on a golf course. If I want to learn how to throw a baseball, I have to get a mitt and a ball and a partner and throw the baseball.

My wife and I want to buy a new home. The home could require us to pay about 80 percent more in housing cost. I can do it. I know I can do it because for the last year, I've paid my mortgage plus an additional 80 percent into a brokerage account. So if that house comes around, there will not be a "I think I can do it . . . " pause, because for the last year, I've done it. Was I comfortable doing it? Hell no, especially not at first. However, after one year of making the payment, it is automatic. I could consider increasing that 80 percent to 100 percent or 110 percent so I'm a little more uncomfortable. One day that uncomfortable payment will become routine.

It is true with every facet of our lives. Run a mile today and it may take you fifteen minutes. Keep running that same mile every other day for a month and on day thirty you'll run that mile in under twelve minutes. Continue another month and that same mile gets done in under ten minutes. The key is getting uncomfortable doing it and keeping at the discomfort. The key is being comfortable being uncomfortable.

When you do hard things, it pays off. When you are running eight-minute miles because you kept at it, you feel healthy and confident. You feel confident because you made a promise to yourself and you kept it. That's the key—we mistakenly get confidence from seeking the approval from others, when we really could be getting that confidence from ourselves. When we feel good about what we're doing, it doesn't matter what another person thinks. You feel confident because you kept a promise to yourself to run every other day and see the benefits from it. You feel confident because you kept the promise to save $25 a day, and after two months you see the benefits of keeping that promise with $1,500 in your savings account.

You Will Not Fail

If you put the work in, you will not fail. If you put the work in, you will get stronger. If you put the work in, tomorrow you will be able to do more than you can do today. If you put the work in, you can accomplish almost anything you want. But you need to put the work in. If you are not afraid of doing the work, you will not fail.

If you are not afraid of failure, you will not fail. Because you'll redefine failure. Failure isn't failure when you get back up and try again. Failure becomes failure when you stop trying. When a baby is learning to walk, they fall over; they will keep falling as they learn to get their balance and gain strength to manage walking. Only if that baby stops trying will they be unable to walk. The consistent try, fail, learn process we went through when learning to walk taught us how to do that. And now, putting together what appeared to be complex functions when we were babies, getting up and walking to a destination is automatic and easy.

Do Not Allow Racism to Be an Excuse to Stop Trying

There are many things that can interfere with our trying, and our mindset around racism is often one of those things. We fail and blame it on racism (and yes, racism may actually be to blame!). But like the baby learning how to walk, we have to pick ourselves up and try again. We fail when we stop trying. Do not allow racism to be the reason you stop trying.

We have certainly been beaten down by centuries of

hatred. That constant beating has pervaded our consciousness. But I challenge you that the constant beating, that constant refrain of "you don't belong," the drumbeat that "you are not enough" stops today. It stops by recognizing it within yourself. It stops by recognizing unconscious limiting beliefs and switching them out with the positive. Be compassionate with yourself—our culture has burdened us with generations of limiting beliefs. For centuries our country told us we were not human. The subconscious belief that we are less than doesn't heal itself overnight.

We are very fortunate to live in this time, in this nation, on our planet. We do not suffer the same systemic racism that our ancestors did. We are not in chains. We are no longer in physical bondage. We have access to education. We have the ability to go to resources and create opportunities. We only need to decide to do it. We only need to intentionally make decisions that will get us to the greatness within rather than unconsciously reacting to circumstances around us and staying put where we are.

Let's honor our ancestors' pain not by constantly reliving it but by thriving in spite of racism. Let's acknowledge their pain by building the greatness they sought. By building the greatness they deserved. Let's acknowledge their pain by taking the opportunity we have to be great. Let's create the lives our ancestors dreamed for us!

Be Unreasonable!

If you knew that you would not fail, what would you want to do?

You wrote down your North Star earlier in the pages of this book. You now need people around you who support your dream. Maybe you want to be a doctor. Surround yourself with people who affirm that goal. It won't be helpful to have people around you who constantly say you'll never be a doctor. Find people who will push you to your goal and support you. They are there.

When I tell you to be unreasonable, please know there is a difference between *unreasonable* and *irresponsible*. The distinction between the two involves work. Unreasonable is coming up with a plan and working toward a specific goal, whereas irresponsible is betting it all on a craps table because a book you read said you will not fail. Let's be clear: when you do the work toward a big goal, even failure brings opportunity.

Though I wanted to write a book, I was waking up daily in the "lawyer" routine. Then one day I listened to that little whisper and started living more intentionally to make that long-deferred dream a reality. And now I sit here writing these words on this page. I don't know where I will end up. The journey that has taken me to this desk writing these words has been amazing. My life was transformed because I listened to the whisper that said, *write a book*. It wasn't necessarily reasonable to listen to that whisper. I had bills to pay, clients to service, payroll to make, play performances and Little League baseball games to attend. But I wrote one page one day. And then another. And as the pages added up over a long, long time, I had the opportunity to live different experiences. I met mentors who walked me through the process. I met agents and publishers and editors and people who were writing books and *New York Times* best-selling authors.

Near the beginning of the adventure of writing a book, I challenged myself by doing my modified Goggins. During that painful walk in my neighborhood, I heard *You will not fail* whispered, and I cried knowing with certainty that was true. At the time, I thought the whisper was talking about the walk. And maybe it was. But what I know to be true today, after working my way to published author, was that the whisper foretold the very moment I write these words. It knew about the people I would meet on this journey and the many awesome experiences I would have. *I will not fail* was not only about those steps, that walk, or that day; it was about life. Today's gratitude is less about the finished book and more about all the many moments that got me here.

I get that telling the world I hear whispers that caused an emotional response can sound a bit . . . irrational. But I want you to listen for your whisper too. Listen for what your heart wants you to do. Because greatness is within you. You deserve greatness. You deserve the small and the big. You deserve all the moments that make your dream real. You deserve the moments when you look around and smile to yourself and say, "I can't believe this is happening!" Go out there and keep moving toward your North Star and enjoy the journey.

You will not fail.

Acknowledgments

WHEN I BEGAN this project, I believed writing a book was a solitary endeavor. I believed the process was one where I sat down at a computer for months, wrote a bunch of words, printed those words, and put red ink to paper. And do that over and over. Although that was much of the process, there are so many people who were essential in creating this book.

Matthew Bivens started the journey with me by helping me build the habit of writing daily with his wonderful advice and keeping me accountable for it. Jon Samnick took the accountability baton and put me in touch with other authors, like Robin Kimball Eisenbeis, who helped keep my fingers on the keyboard. After the habit was built, Jim House gave the book its foundation with a true outline for what I wanted to accomplish. Most importantly, Jim gave me license to write it.

I am truly fortunate to have Blaire Ward in my life. I met her while on this journey, and she believed in the project and me from day one. She was instrumental in continually pulling me out of my comfort zone to get the book's message out to more people. Blaire constantly and consistently has had my back in every facet of building this book from a bunch of words on a page to a living, breathing thing. This book would not exist without her. Blaire introduced me to my agent, Nena Madonia Oshman. Along with Blaire, Nena has been my biggest cheerleader, often putting wind into my sails when I was deflated. This book would not have been published without her as well. Nena's belief in the project helped me have confidence. Both Blaire and Nena forcibly removed me from the lawyer's chair I had grown comfortable in and put me where I wanted to be, in the author's seat.

I have many mentors I've never met who have helped shape this book: Ed Mylett and Lisa Nichols are two voices I hear daily. Their voices are the ones I hear as I strive to get myself closer to the man I want to be. I fall short often. But when I do, it's their voices that get me back up. Another mentor, Lewis Howes, I have had the opportunity to meet. His is another voice I often hear in my head—pushing me to move the ball forward daily.

Dr. Trish Smith is an amazing human. She was instrumental in getting me to acknowledge my power. Whenever I accomplished something hard, I gave her the credit for pushing me. She helped me see that although she assisted me into the water, I was the one who did the work once in.

Leah Lakins edited the many words of a lawyer and sliced and diced those words into something much more readable with far fewer tangents, all while taking care of my ego. Amanda Bauch took those words and edited, questioned, and confirmed to make certain the words on the page matched the words in my head. Adam and Lisa Grimenstein took all those sentences and confirmed they all worked.

Jonathan Merkh of Forefront Books cemented me in my author seat. In my life as a lawyer, I had prepared for depositions, hearings, and trials for decades. It was so refreshing to prepare for my first meeting with Jonathan as an "author" at forty-nine years old. The preparation didn't end at that meeting as the team at Forefront, including Kia Harris, knows full well. This product would not be available without all their hard work.

I would not have been able to put this book together without my team at the office. Lucy Garcia, Lesley Hernandez, Natalia Pineda, Josh Comrov, and Will Tripp were instrumental in this process. This would not have been possible without the day we sat in the conference room when I told them of my dream of writing this book. They all not only cheered me on to accomplish the goal but took on much more work to free up my time to do it.

The Privilege Race could not have been published without my wife, Amy. While she thought I was a little crazy for pursuing this project, she always supported the goal. She took on everything at home so I could manage two full-time jobs: lawyer and author. Without her neither *The Privilege Race* nor Thomas Law would exist. Although it is certainly not always easy, I am very proud of all we've built together. Thank you so very much for being my partner. Life is better with you in it.

And finally, I'm grateful to my children, Sammy and Tali, who inspire me to be a little better every day and still love me when I'm not. Everything I do is for the two of you. I love you more.

Notes

1. "Years of Athletic Achievement," David Goggins, accessed June 8, 2023, https://davidgoggins.com/athletic-achievements/.

2. "4x4x48 Goggins Challenge," David Goggins, accessed September 14, 2023, https://www.gogginschallenge.com/.

3. Cummings Athletics, "Life of Privilege Explained in a $100 Race," YouTube, May 25, 2019, https://www.youtube.com/watch?v =7vR3Oovhi1Q.

4. Aimee Groth, "You're the Average of the Five People You Spend the Most Time With," Business Insider, July 24, 2012, https://www.businessinsider.com/jim-rohn-youre-the-average-of-the-five-people-you-spend-the-most-time-with-2012-7.

5. Allen Lee et al., "Association of Daily Intellectual Activities with Lower Risk of Incident Dementia among Older Chinese Adults," *JAMA Psychiatry* 75, no. 7 (July 2018): 697–703, doi:10.1001 /jamapsychiatry.2018.0657.

6. Rebecca Gross, "Why It Pays to Read," National Endowment for the Arts, January 16, 2015, https://www.arts.gov/stories/blog/2015 /why-it-pays-read.

7. Merriam-Webster, s.v. "privilege," accessed June 9, 2023, https://www.merriam-webster.com/dictionary/privilege.

8. Joseph H. Arguinchona and Prasanna Tadi, "Neuroanatomy, Reticular Activating System," National Center for Biotechnology Information, July 25, 2022, https://www.ncbi.nlm.nih.gov /books/NBK549835/.

9. Tobias van Schneider, "If You Want It, You Might Get It. The Reticular Activating System Explained," Medium, June 22, 2017, https://medium.com/desk-of-van-schneider/if-you -want-it-you-might-get-it-the-reticular-activating-system -explained-761b6ac14e53.

10. Wikipedia, s.v. "kaleidoscope," accessed June 9, 2023, https://en.wikipedia.org/wiki/Kaleidoscope.

11. Ijeoma Oluo, *So You Want to Talk About Race* (New York: Seal Press, 2016), 1.

12. "Niggers in the White House," Theodore Roosevelt Center at Dickinson State University, accessed June 9, 2023, https://www.theodorerooseveltcenter.org/Research /Digital-Library/Record.aspx?libID=o284393.

13. *Sedalia Sentinel,* October 25, 1901.

14. Matthew Delmont, "Why African American Soldiers Saw World War II as a Two Front Battle" *Smithsonian Magazine*, August 24, 2017.

15. Delmont, "Why African American Soldiers Saw World War II."

16. Hilary Herbold, "Never a Level Playing Field: Blacks and the GI Bill," *Journal of Blacks in Higher Education* no. 6 (Winter 1994–1995): 104–8.

17. Amir Vera and Laura Ly, "White Woman Who Called Police on a Black Man Bird-Watching in Central Park Has Been Fired," CNN, May 26, 2020, https://www.cnn.com/2020/05/26/us /central-park-video-dog-video-african-american-trnd/index.html.

18. Ashley May, "Black Yale Student Reported to Police for Sleeping in Her Dorm," *USA Today*, May 10, 2018, https://www.usatoday.com /story/news/nation/2018/05/09/yale-black-graduate-student -police/597101002/.

19. This may be the most important podcast episode I've ever heard, and it changed my life. Lewis Howes, "Lisa Nichols on the Key to Abundance and Success," *The School of Greatness* (podcast), January 18, 2016, https://lewishowes.com/podcast/lisa-nichols.